Which Ad Pulled Best?

Tenth Edition

20 Case Histories on How to Write and Design Ads That Work

Scott C. Purvis

President, Gallup & Robinson, Inc.

McGraw-Hill
Irwin

McGraw-Hill Irwin

WHICH AD PULLED BEST?, TENTH EDITION

Published by McGraw-Hill, a business unit of The McGraw-Hill Companies, Inc., 1221 Avenue of the Americas, New York, NY 10020. Copyright © 2011 by The McGraw-Hill Companies, Inc. All rights reserved. Previous edition © 2003. No part of this publication may be reproduced or distributed in any form or by any means, or stored in a database or retrieval system, without the prior written consent of The McGraw-Hill Companies, Inc., including, but not limited to, in any network or other electronic storage or transmission, or broadcast for distance learning.

Some ancillaries, including electronic and print components, may not be available to customers outside the United States.

 This book is printed on recycled, acid-free paper containing 10% postconsumer waste.

1 2 3 4 5 6 7 8 9 0 QDB/QDB 1 0 9 8 7 6 5 4 3 2 1 0

ISBN   978-0-07-811207-2
MHID 0-07-811207-9

Vice President & Editor-in-Chief: *Brent Gordon*
Vice President EDP/Central Publishing Services: *Kimberly Meriwether David*
Editorial Director: *Paul Ducham*
Publisher: *Douglas Hughes III*
Executive Editor: *Michael Ablassmeir*
Marketing Manager: *Katie Mergen*
Development Editor: *Kelly I. Pekelder*
Project Manager: *Robin A. Reed*
Design Coordinator: *Margarite Reynolds*
Cover Designer: *Mary-Presley Adams*
Senior Photo Research Coordinator: *Jeremy Cheshareck*
Cover Image: *The McGraw-Hill Companies, Inc./Mark Dierker, photographer*
Buyer: *Laura Fuller*
Media Project Manager: *Balaji Sundararaman*
Compositor: *Laserwords Private Limited*
Typeface: *10/12 Times Roman*
Printer: *Quad/Graphics*

All credits appearing on page or at the end of the book are considered to be an extension of the copyright page.

Library of Congress Cataloging-in-Publication Data

Which ad pulled best? : 20 case histories on how to write and design ads that work /
[edited by] Scott C. Purvis. — 10th ed.
     p. cm.
   Includes index.
   ISBN 978-0-07-811207-2 (alk. paper)
   1. Advertising. I. Purvis, Scott C.
HF5823.W467 2010
659.1—dc22

                                              2010031329

Contents

Foreword

What Is Good Advertising?

Whether you are a first-time student or an experienced advertising practitioner, you will have opinions about this question based upon experience, common sense, intuition, and sheer guesswork. Sometimes you will be right and sometimes you will not.

Not all advertising is created equal. Some ads draw us in, inform us, engage us, and even motivate us to change our behavior. Other ads bore us, confuse us, seem to ignore us, or even push us away. To help you understand what good advertising is, this book uses real-world advertising and real-world research to show you what ads are more effective than others and what elements were responsible for their performance. In looking at these examples, you will see that certain principles work to improve performance. You will learn some of the success factors that increase the stopping power of advertisements. You will see advertising techniques that involve and engage readers. You will come to see how fact-based guidelines can organize your thinking better than guesswork and intuition.

Sometimes you will agree and sometimes you may disagree, but you should always remember that successful ads are the result of a creative process—the human mind craves stimulus that is different. No one set of principles is going to replace the need for the insightful ideas and creative expression that are at the foundation of each great advertisement. However, learning to look at advertising through the eyes of the audiences whose favor is so critical to any ad's success will help turn those ideas into more effective communication devices. This book, with its unique approach of using contrasting ad pairs, will help reveal and clarify underlying principles that apply in

practice, not just in theory, while being respectful of a process that is both art and craft.

This tenth edition has been substantially updated. The text has all been updated, and the examples are all new, as are the interviews with some of the leading creative minds in the advertising industry. Scott Purvis wrote and edited this new edition and all the critical analyses in the accompanying *Instructor's Manual.* Mr. Purvis is ideally qualified for this work through his years of experience as a practitioner for one of the major advertising research companies working with many of the leading companies and agencies.

The author wishes to thank Mr. William H. Van Pelt, Jr. for his contribution to this book and his tireless work in selecting the ad pairs and presenting their interesting stories. He also wishes to thank Dr. Sandeep Patnaik for helping to arrange the interviews and editing many of the sections and Ms. Brianne Dawson for working so constructively with the publisher to keep the project moving forward.

The tenth edition of this popular book fits admirably into the list of books we offer practitioners, teachers, and students of advertising. Most of all, it brings real-life experiences to the classroom.

Which Ad Pulled Best? is a teaching aid for students. It consists of this book for students and a guide for instructors. The *Instructor's Manual* is necessary for getting full value from the book because it contains the Answer Key for the ad pairs that are presented; reviewers rate the book highly when they purchase the *Instructor's Manual.* The *Instructor's Manual* is sometimes hard to get, so if you are having difficulty finding it please let the publisher know.

Scott Purvis	*The Editors*
Author	McGraw Hill Books

Consumer Advertisements
Tested by Gallup & Robinson

EXAMPLE	1	2	3	4	5
Page	47	49	51	53	55
Advertiser(s)	Dove	Hyundai Subaru	Andersen Pella	Schick	Zenith Pioneer
Product or Service	Deodorant	Autos	Windows	Razors	Televisions
Publication(s) Used	*Glamour* *Cosmopolitan*	*Men's Health* *Bon Appetit*	*Bon Appetit* *Better Homes and Gardens*	*Allure* *Glamour*	*Men's Health*

Influencing Factors	Symbolism/analogy
	Relevance
	Elements that connect/
	   disconnect
	Giantism
	Say-nothing headlines
		Reader focus/too many
		   elements
		Focus on product
		Sub-illustrations/
		   demonstrations
		Identification
		Indirect headlines
		Specific copy
			Illustrations enhance product
			Borrowed interest vs.
			   competing interest
			Product lost
			Brand identification
				Misdirection
				Product in use
				News
				Demonstration
				Linking ad elements
					Reader orientation
					Direct headlines
					News
					Product focus
					Demonstrations should
					   demonstrate
					Verify claims

EXAMPLE	6	7	8	9	10
Page	57	59	61	63	65
Advertiser(s)	Audi	Pur	Glad	Downy	Crest
Product or Service	Autos	Water Purifier	Trash Bags	Fabric Softener	Toothbrush
Publication(s) Used	*Bon Appetit*	*People* *Better Homes and Gardens*	*Ladies' Home Journal* *Cosmopolitan*	*People*	*Cosmopolitan*

Influencing Factors	Close-up photography
	Distinction
	Blends image and product
	Clear, understandable, logical
	   message
	Identification
		Visual contrast
		Product applied
		Identification
		Clear/obscure comparisons
			Problem-solution
			Misdirection
			Claim support
				Product focus
				Concept imagery
				Say-little copy
				Variety
				Identification
				Picture captions
					Larger-than-life
					   illustrations
					Product details/
					   benefits
					Ordinary-routine
					   illustrations

EXAMPLE	11	12	13	14	15
Page	67	69	71	73	75
Advertiser(s)	Pepcid Tums	Discover	Cottonelle	Reach	Volkswagen
Product or Service	Drugs (Antacid)	Credit Card	Bath Tissues	Toothbrush	Autos
Publication(s) Used	*Ladies' Home Journal* *People*	*People* *Better Homes and Gardens*	*Ladies' Home Journal* *Better Homes and Gardens*	*Cosmopolitan* *People*	*Men's Health* *Self*
Influencing Factors	Product focus General/specific benefit headlines Picture caption Feature demonstration Visual contrast News Mental work	Illustrations with high/low initial interest Mnemonic use of identification Short, direct copy General/unique sales ideas	Weak/hard-working illustration Say-nothing/benefit headlines Identification Short-circuited humor Borrowed interest Reason-why benefit support Hard-to-read/short, direct copy Orientation to topic/product	Lack of focus Elements disconnect Mental work Humor Benefit headline Benefit support Identification	Misdirection Relevance Startling illustrations Elements that connect/disconnect Say-nothing headlines Identification Lack of product benefits

EXAMPLE	16	17	18	19	20
Page	77	79	81	83	85
Advertiser(s)	Dannon	Swiffer WetJet Clorox ReadyMop	DHL	The Susan G. Komen Breast Cancer Foundation	Taco Bell Wendy's
Product or Service	Smoothies	Floor Cleaner	Delivery Service	Non-profit Organization	Fast Food Restaurants
Publication(s) Used	*Cosmopolitan* *Redbook*	*People*	*People*	*Newsweek* *Ladies' Home Journal*	*People*
Influencing Factors	Product focus Reader orientation Concept imagery Specific/general headlines Taste appeal Product benefits	Alliteration—word play Product focus Call-outs/captions Ad elements tied together Simplicity vs. complexity	Positive/negative initial reactions Color as positive concept imagery Say-nothing headlines Lack of reader benefits	Indirection Symbolism Say-nothing headlines Informative copy Problem-solution technique Illustration that conveys the topic Direct, strong headlines	Illustration techniques of exaggeration, concept imagery, call-outs/captions Tongue-in-cheek humor Taste appeal Variety Headline concerns/comments

Principles Demonstrated by Tested Advertisements

Example Number

Ad as a whole
(unity, strong theme, tie-in of elements, devices to attract and hold interest)

1, 3, 4, 6, 9, 11, 13, 14, 17, 18

Copy
(appeals, idea, subject matter, technique)

2, 4, 5, 6, 9, 11, 13, 14, 18, 19

Headline
(importance, techniques, faults, appeals used)

2, 4, 5, 9, 10, 11, 13, 14, 16, 18, 19

Illustration
(symbolism, demonstration, giantism, problem-solution, appeals, relevance)

1, 2, 3, 4, 5, 6, 7, 8, 9, 10, 11, 12, 13, 14, 15, 16, 17, 18, 19, 20

Other devices
(celebrities, variety, humor, branding)

2, 3, 5, 6, 13, 14, 15, 17, 20

List of Advertisers

The Who-What-How of Testing Printed Advertising

The 20 pairs of advertisements you will find in this book were tested by the prominent research organization Gallup & Robinson, Inc. They are all actual ads, tested as part of an ongoing research program, and the lessons that are drawn are regularly used by many practitioners to make decisions about and improve their advertising. In the following material you will learn about the research method employed in the testing. You will learn about other research techniques that are used today to evaluate and improve advertising effectiveness. Then there will be a general discussion of research methods, criticisms and virtues, and guidelines for advertisers and agencies that stem from research findings. This will be followed by a series of interviews with some of the leading minds involved in the creation of advertising, who will talk about how they think about and create advertising in general and print advertising in particular.

ADVERTISING RESEARCH IS A RELATIVE NEWCOMER

In the early days of advertising there was almost no research—keeping records of inquiries produced by advertisements was about all there was. Then came the depression, when cost-conscious advertisers demanded to know the factors behind the success or failure of advertisements. Thus, you might say that meaningful scientific research began in the 1930s.

Advertising research has been controversial from the start. It is *still* a subject of debate among advertisers, advertising agency people, and researchers themselves; there is no one system on which all agree. Still, a number of measurement areas have won general acceptance and many areas of what had been executional guesswork for the early advertisers have been eliminated. From research, we now have a clearer sense of the types of questions that should be asked and the principles that, if followed, give advertisers much more assurance of obtaining good readership, communication, inquiries, and/or sales.

Part of the controversy about copy research derived from its having been initially conceived as a posttest. After the advertising had been developed by their agencies, companies would measure how well it did while it was being run. Measurement results and learning from the posttest were then used to improve the next round of ads.

This often put advertisers and especially ad agencies in the postion of needing to defend their work-product with their clients after considerable money had been invested in developing and running a campaign. Over the years, the posttest model of measurement led to increasing dissatisfaction with the research process and vocal criticism of its measures. This has dissipated in more recent times as technologies enabled research to be conducted earlier in the ad development process and led to more learning about how the measures work.

Today, advertising research is well-integrated into the business process used by most leading advertisers to manage their advertising investment and make it more effective. Pretesting, where the advertising is tested before it has run or in a rough, prefinished form, has become the preferred model for copy research. The Internet has shrunk the time to do research and reduced its costs. This makes it a valuable tool for sorting through concepts or executional elements. Finished or near-finished ad testing is often additionally done to qualify an ad for in-market release. The type of research that is done can vary across companies, depending on their products and the objectives of their advertising and research.

THE GALLUP & ROBINSON IMPACT METHOD

The ad examples that are used in this book were tested under Gallup & Robinson's Magazine Impact Research Service (MIRS). The key objective of MIRS is to assess performance of individual ads or campaigns in the context in which they are/will be exposed. Because context influences response, by having people see ads in the context of actual ads and editorial, the system provides the most "real-world" assessment of effectiveness available. MIRS measures have been proved to be predictive of in-market performance.

To accomplish its key objective, the MIRS system enables users to assess their own and competitive advertising within the context of actual consumer and business magazines either as the ad naturally apears or as it has been tipped into a test issue. In addtion, respondents read the magazine at their home or office as they normally would, rather than in a lab or test environment. The sample size for a typical consumer survey is approximately 150 men and/or women, ages 18 and older. Studies can also be done among specific target audiences. Qualified readers are located by continuous household canvass in metropolitan areas geographically dispersed across the United States. Respondents must also be regular magazine readers and qualify by having read two of the last four issues of the test magazine or others in the same classification, but they must not have read the current issue.

The test magazine is placed at the respondent's home, and the respondent is interviewed by telephone the following day. Readers are given no advance information of the nature of the interview but are requested to read the magazine on the day of placement and not to read it on the day of the interview.

During the follow-up telephone interview, respondents are asked preliminary questions to determine readership. A list of ads appearing in the magazine is read, and respondents are asked which ad they remember. For each ad the respondent claims to recall, he or she is asked a series of open- and closed-ended questions. These are called the *impact questions* and include:

1. You may be familiar with other ads for Brand X, but thinking only of this issue, please describe the ad as you remember it. What did the ad look like and say?

2. What sales points or reasons for buying did they show or talk about?

3. What did you learn about the (product/service) from this ad?

4. What thoughts and feelings went through your mind when you looked at the ad?

5. The advertiser tried to increase your interest in its (product/service). How was your buying interest affected?

- Increased considerably
- Increased somewhat
- Not affected
- Decreased somewhat
- Decreased considerably

6. What was in the ad that makes you say that?

The impact questions yield a rich quality of verbatim testimony that is used to prove readership and understand people's reactions to the ad and what it communicates. The interview also produces a variety of measurements of advertising effectiveness. Two of the most important, and the ones that will be used in the examples in this book, are:

1. *Intrusiveness/Recall (Proved Name Registration)*—the percentage of respondents who can accurately describe the ad the day following exposure. This measure is an indicator of the ad's ability to break through the clutter and command attention. For comparative purposes, the percentages are adjusted for space/color, unit cost, and magazine type.

2. *Persuasion (Favorable Buying Attitude)*—the distribution of respondent statements of how the ad affected purchase interest. This measure is a relative indicator of the ad's ability to persuade. For corporate or cause advertising, the persuasion measure indicates the extent to which the ad made a strong case for the advertiser.

It is important to note that recall and persuasion measure different aspects of communication and are not correlated with each other. An ad that is effective at causing people to stop and look at it may not be effective in enhancing positve attitudes about the brand, and visa versa. The use of superfluous sex in advertising is an example of a technique that is often effective in getting attention, but usually not effective in enhancing brand attitutdes.

In addition to evaluative information of recall and persuasion discussed above, a series of additional evaluative and diagnostic questions about how people react to the advertising itself and to the brand is also asked of people who remember the ad or who do not remember it but were re-exposed for it during the telephone interview. Companies are usually interested in knowing what the ads communicate, how people feel about the ads, whether the ads are engaging, and whether they reinforce positive imagery about the brand. Each interview concludes with a series of classification questions.

Measures themselves need to have benchmarks in order to assess what they mean. Being six feet tall means something different when it it is looked at in the context of men versus women. In advertising research different product categories have different interest levels (generally more people are interested in food advertising than they are in mutual fund advertising). For this reason, Gallup & Robinson uses a highly developed database of product category-specific norms. The extensive coverage of MIRS yields a wide range of product-specific and gender-specific normative data.

Each MIRS report on client and/or competitive advertisements contains the following:

- Copy of the tested ad
- Intrusiveness (proved name registration) measure
- Idea communication profile
- Persuasion (favorable buying attitude) measure
- Ad liking
- Ad engagement
- Ad diagnostics
- Brand attitudes
- Standard and customized evaluative and diagnostic measures
- Norms
- Verbatim testimony for the ad
- Sample characteristics

The report is accompanied by an interpretative summary that recaps key findings and recommendations.

MIRS pretests ads in actual magazine publications by enabling advertisers to "tip into" a test issue. With today's printing technologies, ad concepts or near-finished ads can be quickly and inexpensively created and then inserted into most magazines so that the test ad appears as if it ran naturally. Most MIRS testing today is done for pretesting and uses the tip-in technique.

Gallup & Robinson pioneered many of the research techniques that have become standard for helping advertisers and agencies evaluate the effectiveness of their advertising in the marketplace and gain a better understanding of how audiences process advertising messages. The systems have been used to evaluate over 120,000 print ads and 60,000 television commercials.

OTHER FORMS OF AD RESEARCH

In addition to online surveys or in-context techniques like MIRS, companies employ a variety of other research designs depending on where they are in the ad development process and what the objectives of their advertising are. Research is done before any ads are developed to learn about the audience and their needs. It is also done to get rough feedback about possible ad concepts or ideas. As specific ad concepts are developed, alternative concepts or ads are often evaluated individually to identify which one or ones resonate most strongly with the audience and how they can be improved. There are three main ways in which this research is done.

Qualitative Research

One popular form of research has involved simply getting together to talk about the issues, advertising ideas or concepts that the advertiser is learning more about. The interaction may take place among small groups (typically called *focus groups*) or individually (typically called *in-depth one-on-one interviews* or IDIs). In both cases, a structured but also flexible conversation is held to gain insight about the target audience's reaction to the advertising led by skillful moderators or interviewers. They typically employ a series of open- and closed-ended questioning techniques that help the consumer express his or her feelings about the advertising and the kinds of associations it engenders. In addition to straight question and answer approaches, these might be obtained through psychological testing that uses projective techniques such as free word association, sentence completion, or picture responses.

Out of the foregoing comes an appreciation of how the person thinks about the product or brand, and how the intended advertising communicates to the reader. A key strength of this approach is that the advertiser and its ad agency are able to listen together to what the consumer is saying, which provides an unvarnished and real-time sense of the thoughts and feelings that the consumer is sharing. A key weakness of the approach is that groups may think about things differently than individuals do and they are likely not representative of the market as a whole. Also, assessments of what the person said can be very subjective and it is often possible to hear what you want to hear.

Qualitative research investigators often proceed from the assumption that they do not know what their research may uncover. Questions are deliberately nondirected with the purpose being to draw out new insights that the advertiser or agency may not have already considered. In addition, subrational behavior, drives, fears and desires can often lie behind people's reactions to the product or situation being studied. Out of the qualtative approach may come ideas that respondents cannot or will not give in the course of an ordinary telephone interview.

Prompted by the feeling that asking people directly how they feel about something will fail to uncover how they really feel underneath, some qualitative research attempts to drill into the subconscious or preconscious level of motivations. Often, trained psychologists listen to and analyze responses for their meaning. This form of research, which was once heavily practiced, is enjoying a resurgence in appeal as more neurophysiological evidence demonstrates the value of emotions in shaping cognititve thought and purchase decision making.

Quantitative Research

Quantitative testing is thought to be a more objective form of research because it is built on the science of survey research. Here, the advertising researcher is often less interested in uncovering something new than in assessing the extent to which it is true. For example, during a qualitative study, the objective might be to develop insights that can be used for what an ad should say, while in a quantitative study, the objective might be to determine the percentage of people who understand or agree with the insight.

Quantitative studies use more rigorous sampling procedures than qualitaitve studies. Both kinds of studies attempt to talk to people who represent the market of interest, but focus groups tend to talk to fewer of them than quantitative studies do. A focus group may have 6–10 people in it, although often more than one group is studied. Quantitative copy test studies are usually conducted among 100–200 people. These substantially larger numbers mean that the results from quantitative studies have more stability, less sampling error and are more likely predictive of the population being studied. Quantitative studies

are conducted in a one-on-one framework (one interviewer talking to one respondent at a time) so respondents' opinions are offered without being influenced by what others in a group may feel. Quantitative studies use more closed-ended questions, which force the respondent to be clearer about what he or she means and are less subject to ambiguity when being interpreted and discussed. Analytically, quantitative studies can be more powerful because they are amenable to statistical analyses.

In addition to the in-context design that MIRS is based on, another form of quantitative copy testing is based on a forced-exposure technique. Here, the advertising is presented to people, either by itself or in a context of other ads, who are asked to look at it and then asked quesitons about what they saw immediately or shortly after exposure. The forced-exposure design is most effective when the key research objective is to understand what the ad communicates and what a person's overall reaction to it is likely to be. The MIRS design is considered better research practice when a key objective is to understand "attentioning," the ad's ability to break through and get noticed, a particularly important part of print advertising effectiveness, and retained communication, what stays with the person over time.

One of the most important recent developments in quantitative testing is the increasing use of the Internet to find samples and conduct interviews. This technology enables studies to be conducted significantly more quickly (in a matter of days rather than weeks) and for substantially lower costs. The downside of this design is that the stimulus is presented over the computer, usually in a smaller size than how it is actually seen. Most online designs also present the ads using the forced-expsoure design, adding to a less realistic exposure context. And there are still questions to be answered about the representativeness of people who participate in online surveys. Online testing is an excellent solution for concept and rough ad testing, but it can be less effective when the objecitve is to understand how the ad is likely to perform in the real world across the full communication dynamic.

Response Testing

Response tests are made by keeping track of the changes in attitudes or behavior that the advertising produces, typically in awareness, favorable attitudes, number of inquires, clicks, or direct sales produced by each advertisement. When the purpose of a campaign is not simply to generate an immediate response, advertisers often track ongoing awareness levels and attitudes about the brand. Interviews are conducted among people to ascertain how, for example, their levels of awareness, knowledge, and opinions about the brand change during the course of a campaign. When the purpose of the advertising is to generate immediate action, an advertiser can run an ad against one group of people and see how many people are interested enough to follow up on the offer. A second advertisement making a different offer or using a different executional approach is run for a different group of people and resulting inquiries again counted. The results from the two advertisements or campaigns can then be compared on the basis of inquiries produced.

In order to be certain that results come from a specific advertisement, the advertiser may insert a key number in the coupon or in a paragraph near the bottom of the advertisement in which the offer appears, or place a cookie in a user's browser and suggest that respondents take advantage of the offer. "Keys" have taken many forms, such as routing numbers, post office box numbers, telephone numbers, cookies, and landing pages, and can be changed each time a different advertisement is run. This approach is often used as part of the measurement plan for an Internet campaign where "clicks" are easily, automatically, and often, tracked.

Responses are tallied according to the advertisement that produced them as they come in. Records are kept of how many inquiries are produced by each advertisement run in each different medium. Such records show not only which advertisements are producing the most inquiries but which media and publications as well.

A record can also show which inquiries are most valuable in developing sales. When direct response advertisers get an inquiry (say, a request for more infomation), they follow up with literature designed to make a sale. Then, as sales are made, they relate the number and size of orders back to the inquiry and the advertisement that made the first contact. In this way, advertisers keep track not only of which advertisements produce the most inquiries but also which locate the best prospects—quite often there is a difference.

Although sales do not necessarily match inquiry returns, and inquiries alone do not say much about the far greater percentage of people who saw but did not respond to the ad, such returns can be a good indication of the interest developed by a given advertisement. Comparisons of responses produced by different advertisements also indicate the relative interest created by each. This is especially true if some qualifying device is used in an advertisement, such as requiring people asking for the booklet or sample to pay out some token amount in order to obtain the offer. Such a requirement tends to discourage those not truly interested.

Sales Tests

For many advertisers, even those not in the direct-response business, sales provide the real test of effectiveness. Publishers, for example, have found it profitable to sell directly through published advertising, and a number of products elicit sales directly through long television commercials and the Internet. Additionally, with today's data capture capabilities at mass retailers and supermarkets, companies are increasingly able to infer the sales consequences of their advertising. Increasingly sophisticated forms of statistical analyses are able to parse the data to identify the marketing communications components that have contributed to it most. Because such studies tend to be time-consuming and costly, they have not replaced the need for copy testing.

A NOTE ON EMOTION

During the past 20 years, advancements in the fields of neuroscience and behavioral economics have led to better brain research technology and understanding of the role of emotions in decision making. Indeed, many feel that there has been a paradigm shift to the point that abstract constructs or theories about information processing and decision making can no longer be developed simply by rationally based parsing of data and without grounding in the workings of the brain and its emotion-based processing. Discoveries of emotional and cognitive processes and circuits in the brain are revealing almost daily the basic and important elements that determine human behavior. Neuroscience is showing us that processing of messages is often subconscious, implicit, and intuitive. Behavioral economics is showing us that how the consumer *feels* about the product or media can be a better predictor of consumer behavior than what the consumer *thinks* about the product or media. This increased focus on emotional/nonrational processing, and even the more complex integration with cognition, is teaching us that emotion is critical to how we think; it organizes and energizes one's response to the environment, and therefore underlies and drives attitudes and behaviors. Interestingly, one of the offshoots of this work is a general confirmation of the validity of the long-standing copy testing measures. Positive correlations have been found between the new physiological measures of response and recall (and its relationship to memory) and liking (and its relationship to affect).

A NOTE ABOUT MAGAZINE ADS

Print advertising has undergone signficant change since the publication of our last edition of this book. The Internet has become a major source of news, information, and entertainment for many people. In addition, many new media have emerged. And where there are audiences, there will be advertisers. Where print used to be perenially a strong number two to TV, now its overall position is in decline and its future is less certain.

Regardless of its future, print remains an important entry point for learning about advertising:

1. It is big. Nine in ten adults read magazines.

2. While the term "print" has usually lumped newspapers and magazines together, the negative influence of the Internet on magazines has been relatively mild compared to its influence on newspapers.

3. Print is a powerful medium for the creators of advertising. Perhaps more than any other medium, it allows the creative complete control over the content. Thus the advertiser is better able to ensure the faithful translation of his or her vision into tangible form.

4. Print uniquely allows for the creation of one total iconic image to represent and register the meaning of the brand.

5. Print ads contain all of the same elements of the other media forms, so understanding print enables a person to understand the key elements of all other messaging.

6. Print is an efficient way to reach key target audiences, who often consider the advertising to be a more integrated part of the reading experience than is the case in other media.

COPY TESTING DOESN'T REPLACE JUDGMENT

Copy testing is about what goes on in the human mind and how the mind can be influenced by external inputs like advertising to make decisions and take action. As such, and like all attitudinal research, the results are incomplete because understanding how the human mind works is still an evolving investigation. Also, measurement always contains error and that is especially so in survey research where relatively small groups of people are sampled in order to draw conclusions about a large population.

In addition, each form of research has its own particular source of potential errors. Some of the issues that can affect copy testing reliability are the following:

1. Differences in testing design. An ad tested in one experimental design can perform differently than the same ad tested in another design. An ad that does well in a forced-exposure setting will not necessarily do well in a real-world setting.

2. Differences in the media used. An ad tested in one magazine, program, or clutter environment can perform differently than an ad tested in another magazine or program. That is because the enivronment in which an ad appears influences how people respond to it. Therefore, it is important that media context issues be considered in any design.

3. Differences across people. Some people "consume" advertising differently than other people. Variations in reading habits, receptivity mood, and buying habits; differences in the general interest in the product or service offered; and dissimilarities according to the day of the week or time of the year can influence results. For example, people generally pay more attention to food advertising than to mutual fund advertising or may be more receptive to buying something during Christmas than Labor Day. However, neither is true of all people, all time. Therefore, it is important people be representative of the audience the advertiser intends to research, both in audience demographics and attitudes.

4. Differences across samples. If you ask 100 people a question, they may give you a different average anwer than if you ask another 100 people that same question. This can be especially so if the sample is a 10-person focus group or a 200-person online panel. Statistics is one of the tools that enables researchers to estimate how much error there is for a given sample size. Therefore, it is important to look for natural variations resulting simply from the law of averages

Depending on the degree to which these factors are present in a copy test, results can differ widely for an ad tested under one set of conditions and the same ad tested under another set of conditions. Thus, most copy testing systems ensure that these factors are kept constant between two ad studies. In addition, better research practice would call for the ads to be tested as close to finish as possible, in a real world context; in the same class of magazines and appearing in the same position in the magazine.

Researchers often balance the need to test under real-world versus artificial condtions. Real-world testing provides results that are most predictive of real-world performance but can have greater variability. Artificial conditions can be less influenced by external factors, but the test results themselves are more artificial. Using real-world conditions with controlled exposure conditions is the best testing protocol.

Copy testing is a tool for better decision making. It is not a replacement for judgment. As in all research, results should be looked at critically, reconciled with other learning about the ad, and then termpered by experience before final decisions are made.

DIFFERENT MEASURES MEASURE DIFFERENT PARTS OF THE COMMUNICATION DYNAMIC

Many measures are used in copy testing. Some measures have more value, depending on the objetives of the advertising. Some ads may be more about acquiring new customers, so measures about changes in purchase intent are usually included. Other ads may be more about trying to get existing customers to use the produce more, so questions about increased buying interest are usually included. Other ads are about generating awareness, so questions about branding can be key. And other ads are about improving or reinforcing the reputation or image of the brand, so questions about attitudes, liking, and engagement become central. Of course, most ads have multiple objectives, so most companies use multiple measures as part of their copy testing program.

Over the years there has been considerable research about which measure is the best single measure of copy performance. Initially there were two main camps, depending on the two dominant copy testing systems. Recall-based systems were primarily interested in whether an ad or commercial broke through the clutter and could be remembered 24 hours after exposure. Persuasion-based systems were primarily interested in whether exposure to an ad resulted in a change in purchase likelihood among readers or viewers. There was much acriminious and self-serving

debate in favor of one solution over the other, with some advertisers tending to prefer one approach over the other based on their experience. Companies like Procter and Gamble and Kraft were big users of recall, and Unilever was a big user of persuasion.

In the 1980s the Advertising Research Foundation (ARF) conducted a study that was funded by leading advertisers, agencies, and Gallup & Robinson to establish which measures were most predictive of sales. Five pairs of commercials for established packaged goods companies were copy-tested by various copy testing measures. The commercials were all run in-market using split-cable technology where, unknown to the respondents, one household would see one commercial and another household would see another commercial of the pair. Respondents were then tracked over time about the products they purchased.

The ARF study analyzed how predictive individual copy testing measures were of actual sales activity. The conclusions were both reassuring and surprising. Reassuringly, the ARF Copy Research Validity Project found that copy quality alone was one of the key drivers of sales and that individual measures were predictive of copy quality. Surprisingly, the two most predictive measures of copy quality were recall and ad liking. Both measures were more predictive than any of the persuasion measures, particulary pre- and postpurchase intent shift, which was less predictive than post-only persuasion measures like brand rating. Recall and ad liking together correctly predicted 93% of the outcomes. The study has a lot of caveats, but the consequences of it are that today, most companies use multiple measures of performance, usually some form of recall and some form of effect (liking, persuasion, and/or engagement) in their copy testing programs. This is evidence, too, that persuasion is a more permanent, and therefore a more desirable, consequence of advertising than liking.

GUIDELINES FOR COPY REVEALED BY COPY TESTING

No single formula works successfully all the time in creating successful advertisements. Indeed, the challenge of outstanding creative advertising is to not become hamstrung by conventional thinking. Rules and historical artifacts often lead to stereotypical executions, and are a source of performance weakness. On the other hand, ads that are creative for their own sake often suffer on performnace. The general guidelines that copy testing have given rise to simply indicate what has worked in the past and what is *likely* to work in the future. Because ads are intended to communicate business messages, these building blocks of effective advertising, when heeded by the creative team, will result in techniques and approaches that will be more right than wrong.

Great ads balance the need to be different and distincitve with the need to convey enough familiarity to be inviting and accessible to read. Following are some of the guildelines that have been developed through copy research.

1. *Offer a major benefit.* Benefits take different forms—a product most people want; a product easy to get; a product that helps you to feel better about yourself or others; a product worth paying for; a product priced as low as possible. Help people understand the benefit in terms of its rational and emotional appeal.

2. *Be specific; make the message easy to see and read.* Despite all the findings of copy testing, this advice is frequently ignored, even by sophisticated advertisers and advertising agencies. Picture the benefit clearly, simply, and as large as possible. It should be presented with easy-to-grasp language— simple, convincing prose supported by a layout that ties in and is equally easy to follow. Many of the more mechanical "rules" of advertising effectivness are often more usefully thought of as expressing this principle. For example, some research findings conclude the reverse print (which uses light-colored fonts) should be avoided. What they are really saying is that reverse print should be avoided when it makes the ad hard to read. When reverse print is used over a light or varigated background that is often the case, but when it is used over a dark background it can be unproblematic.

3. *Establish audience identity.* Make it easy for viewers to see themselves in pictures on the screen or in illustrations in the publication. The copy, too, should involve the audience by giving ideas on how to use or profit from the benefit. In short, be inclusive. Establish a relationship between the audience and the ad.

4. *Attract by being new.* Advertising's strongest weapon is news—new products, new uses for products, new benefits. Accordingly, the most powerful advertisements include something novel in the benefit that offers new reasons to buy or new ways to understand why the benefit is of value. Even old ideas presented in a new way can be compelling.

Successful advertisements fit the news approach by using action pictures, modern settings, image-laden nouns, active language written in present tense, and word pictures.

5. *Be believable.* Implicit in the concept of a brand is the idea of trust. The strength of a brand is directly related to the trust that the consumer has in what it stands for. Extravagant claims, brag and boast copy, slick phrases, and misleading illustrations damage an ad's credibility. Sadly, when different vocations are rated according to honesty, advertising people are rated near or at the bottom. This influences how people think about advertising and its overall effectiveness. To achieve believability, do not make unreasonable claims. Avoid the blue-sky approach in describing benefits. Supply proof for what you say. In pictures and illustrations, show the product realistically; do not doctor it so that there is a difference between the product in the advertising and that in the hand. This same observation also holds for what you say in the copy.

6. *Stress what is unique.* Advertising people express uniqueness as a "point of difference" or "USP"—unique selling proposition. Both terms refer to an attractive feature available solely in the advertised product and/or promoted as an exclusive benefit. The difference could be tangible, such as performance, styling, price, size, or ease of use, or intangible, such as using the product might influence how your are perceived by others. Usually the first question you should have when asked to write about a product or service, is: "What is different or distinctive about it?" That is the starting point of the creative process.

7. *Be fresh.* Even more than being creative, an ad should be fresh. People tire of seeing the same stale stories, images, or techniques. Fresh is something somewhat unexpected, but not too unexpected. Merely being fresh, however, is wasted without creditable and unique content.

8. *Provide a clear point of entry.* Use a layout that makes it clear to the readers where you want them to begin. Make sure the reader gets to your main message as soon as possible as many readers will only go so far and no farther before they move on.

9. *Brand.* Make sure the reader knows who you are. And do not be shy about it. Unless the ad associates the messaging with your brand name, there is little business value in an ad.

10. Reward the reader for his or her time. Whether it is new learning, reinforced conviction, or some form of purposeful entertainment, the readers should feel rewarded for the time they have spent with your ad. That will enhance how they thinks of you and leaves him or her more open to future messages.

What you have read in the foregoing only touches upon the generalities stemming from copy research.

Still, each of these points is important and, if followed, will help you avoid some of the most common mistakes in writing copy and designing ads. Remember though, more than any of the mechanical elements of an ad, what matters most in an ad is not any of its particular parts, but its creative whole.

Why "It's the Benefit" and How to Make It Work

The more impressive the benefit, the greater the result in advertising. That is the main conclusion that stands out in this analysis of advertisements compared in the *Which Ad Pulled Best?* examples. Whatever the example, the difference in the way people react to the advertisements can be traced back to the benefit: its believability, its uniqueness, how important it was, and how compelling it was presented to the people who read the advertisements.

Benefits take many forms. They can be tangible or intangible. They can be reason-based or they can be emotion-based. It takes insight to determine the key benefits of a product. It may require systematic research or the more hazardous trial and error of years of experience to narrow the possible benefits down to the ones that are of the essence to a product's competitive advantage. Furthermore, it takes skill to transmit the benefit idea through all the media and techniques of mass communication, keeping it fresh over time.

When benefits are presented in the following ways, advertisements will, in general, produce better results.

1. Name the benefit. Be specific about it.

The more specific advertisements are the more successful ones. This holds true regardless of the type of publication, audience, or product. As examples:

- An advertisement headlined *Low-cost steam—Shop assembled and ready to use* pulled twice the readers that *Steam That Satisfies* did.

- Similarly, of two advertisements illustrating the same foldaway table for stores, the advertisement headlined *Move up to $100 in iced watermelons in 8 sq. ft. of space* sold 3½ times as much merchandise as the one headlined *8 square feet of dynamic display.*

- An offer for a recipe book that included a detailed table of contents drew 136% more returns than the offer that merely announced 64 pages packed with methods, recipes, and tips on freezing and canning.

- Of two advertisements run under the heading *Relax in Daks,* the one in which the body copy described these slacks most specifically with "No belt, no pressure around the middle. Hidden sponge rubber pads keep a polite but firm grip on your shirt" produced six times as many inquiries as the vaguer "They're self-supporting, shirt-controlling, and leave the body perfectly free."

- For a self-sealing envelope, the U.S. Envelope Company tested eight different headlines. Some of the approaches were *So sanitary; Novel; Different; Better; Humid weather never affects.* However, by far, the most successful headline read *Avoid licking glue,* which was the most tangible, specific benefit.

The headline, though, does not work alone. *It's amazing! It's sensational! It's exclusive!* This received twice as much response as *How to become a popular dancer overnight.* Although the winning headline consisted of generalities, the advertisement itself contained a specific element that the other did not—a detailed diagram of one of the basic dance steps. A strong visual can save a poor headline. Strong copy, alone, cannot.

2. The product is the big benefit. Tell what it will do.

The more successful advertisements lay greater emphasis on the product. Greater product emphasis coincides with greater success. This can be demonstrated in a variety of ways:

- Two advertisements were headlined *How to get good pictures for sure.* In one advertisement was a large illustration of the camera. It received nearly twice as many inquiries as an ad with the same headline that pictured an attractive man and woman gazing admiringly at the very small camera in their hands. In the first advertisement, the product was the hero and held center stage.

- *Amazing new low-priced electric sprayer for home use makes painting easy* sold 66% more sprayers than did the more humanly interesting *Now Tom does every home painting job himself.* This is because the first headline focuses on the product. What is true of visual emphasis is also true of headline-idea emphasis.

- The catchy but not readily grasped headline *Cool heads in hot spots won't let you down* lost overwhelmingly to the straightforward *Copper's blue ribbon ventilators for workers' safety, health, comfort, efficiency.* While this headline won't win any writing awards, it does focus unmistakably on the product.

Other factors may negate somewhat the effect of product emphasis. An example is that of two advertisements for the same manufacturer, one of which was headlined *Thatcher's 98 years of heating experience means greater comfort at lower cost.* A stark, cold feeling was conveyed by illustrations of four different pieces of heating equipment. The headline for the second advertisement was *Indoor weather made-to-order without lifting your finger.* Here were shown a man and woman in an attractively decorated room, along with a subordinate illustration that featured the one piece of heating equipment needed to provide this "indoor weather." This second advertisement, which pulled three times as many responses, is not only more specific and more humanly interesting, but it also gives more evidence of the benefit to be attained by actual use.

Another example of exceptions to emphasis on product is furnished by a pair of advertisements for Koppers, a global chemical and materials company. One is a highly technical discussion of the structure and physical properties of the product. The other, more successful, advertisement, while containing the technical information, features a different approach: Under a photograph of a piece of soap, a man's shirt, and a plastic dish is the headline *Make them whiter and brighter with Koppers (products).*

3. Keep your advertisements simple. Make it easy for consumers to visualize the benefit.

In most respects, simpler advertisements are consistently more successful. In addition to looking at simplicity as being synonymous with ease, one can consider it an antonym of complexity. In this sense, those advertisements having a single rather than a multiple focus come out ahead.

Consider an example from Eastman Kodak. An ad was divided into four sections. The main headline was *See what you can do with your present equipment.* Each of the four sections featured a different company product. Another issue of the same publication presented an Eastman Kodak advertisement headlined *Because photography is accurate to the last detail.* This was illustrated with a group of mechanical drawings. The copy story was "The magic of photography turns hours of costly drafting room time into a minute-quick job of utmost accuracy." This second advertisement attracted more than twice the readers as the first one. Why should this be? The first advertisement was dramatic in its layout, but it made the reader decide on which section to direct attention and on which story to concentrate. Very few readers will go through all four stories. The second ad guided readers quickly to what the advertiser wanted them to know through a single, simple, integrated story.

Similarly, an advertisement headlined *Great new insurance plan pays hospital, surgical expenses* did not offer as many benefits as the alternative version, *Now great new insurance plan offers you protection for hospital, surgical, and/or doctors' bills and/or lost income.* Yet the former, simpler advertisement pulled twice as many inquiries as the latter advertisement, indicating that it is a mistake to tell too much.

This principle still holds even in very small advertisements. A small, one-column advertisement illustrated with only a large bottle read *On our anniversary we're offering you Welch's Grape Juice at a new low price.* When, to this single theme, the company added a party flavor—children in the illustration wearing party hats and the headline *We are playing host to the nation on our anniversary with the greatest price reduction in Welch's history*—it lost readership.

Simplicity also results from unity of concept when a single theme is developed in headline, artwork, and copy. Two advertisements run for a perforator by Cummins Business Machines offer examples. One had a charming illustration of a young mother putting a cookie jar high on a shelf, out of the reach of her mischievous-looking young son. The headline read *Mr. President—remove opportunity before—not after—fraud.* The second advertisement had no true illustration. On a bold background in white letters made of dots, as if done by a perforator, was the headline *You can't erase a hole. These tiny holes can save you from serious loss.* In the first advertisement the analogy between the kind and thoughtful mother and the kind and thoughtful employers, each looking out for those dependent upon them, is not far-fetched. But in the second and far more successful advertisement, no inferences, however apt, have to be drawn between separate concepts—the entire advertisement consists of one simple, clearly developed idea. Also, the language of the first advertisement is less specific—necessarily so, because a detailed discussion of cookie jars would bear little relation to the perforator being advertised. The point is, then, that not only the simplicity of any single concept, but also the relationship between the product and the consumer, makes the benefit evident.

Visual cues add to simplicity as well. For example, for advertisers seeking direct replies, advertisements that include an illustrated coupon, thus making it easier for consumers to take action, receive a greater response than those without a coupon for reply that merely talk about where the inquiry should be sent.

4. Emphasize the benefit as much as possible. Use large space, up to a point.

Small-space advertisements can work very well. Talk to the average creative person, however, and you will soon find that he or she prefers to work with larger space units. In the larger space you can tell readers more about what the product can do for them. You can use a larger illustration to show more clearly what the product is and how it works. You can use more text material to tell why it is worth the purchase price. You can use larger type to make the copy easier to read and give the headline more impact. A more forceful overall impression can be made by increasing size alone.

Of a group of advertisements almost identical except for size, the larger ones will almost always do as well or better than the smaller versions. However, this rule applies only up to a point. The cost per reader for inquiries or sales is often higher for large advertisements, especially those that use size only for size's sake.

Large space will not work wonders if the content of the advertisement is poor. Technique might also be a factor causing a smaller advertisement to outpull a larger one. "Technique," in this instance, may refer to

such factors as stronger headlines, more clever themes, or more striking, attention-getting illustrations.

Evidence of the efficiency of smaller advertisements is provided in detail by the *Reader's Digest,* which naturally has an interest in convincing advertisers that their smaller advertisements can compete with bigger versions in magazines of conventional size. Although the *Digest* research is impressive, there are in many advertisers' minds distinct visual advantages in working in larger formats.

5. Do not obscure the benefit. The cute, the catchy, or the tricky may not work.

Being cute, catchy, or tricky is subordinate to conveying consumer benefits. Example: A transit card showing a squirrel saying *Take chances? Not me. I'm saving today* lost out to a more direct, more product-oriented card picturing a man saying *My bank—to 1,700,000 Canadians.*

Then, too, there was the lack of success of a comic strip treatment used by a maker of medical supplies such as adhesives, bandages, and back plasters. In tests against three different conventional advertisements, one of which was all type, the comic strip approach was a distant loser. Comic strip illustrations for advertisements about shaving and house painting also showed up badly. The lesson is that a technique associated predominantly with entertainment is often not suitable for selling certain types of products.

This does not mean that the catchy picture or phrase should summarily be rejected—on the contrary, reader-stopping headlines and tricky illustrations have been outstandingly successful. Without such advertising there would be a gray sameness to advertising s a whole. That is the reason there's room for the "different" approach used by the Franklin Institute. When it changed formats from a conventional approach to an offbeat one, the difference in results was striking. In the conventional display advertisement, the headline said *Work for Uncle Sam.* This was far outshone by an advertisement that imitated a classified ad in which the small type was encircled. *Get on Uncle Sam's payroll* was given a bold, black line pointing to a coupon offering further information. This was an appropriate, simple way to sell a training course.

6. Get personal about the benefit, but do not get personal without a purpose.

Formal, impersonal, and passive phraseology is generally less than desirable for mass advertising. You are reminded constantly by copy experts to be—in most advertising—personal and informal. Still, being personal is not always the key to interest and readership. For instance, an Eastman Kodak headline *Because photography is accurate to the last detail* is less personal but was more successful than the one beginning *See what you can do with. . . .*

Of course, the advertiser should always consider the individual circumstances of the target reader. The "be personal" advice takes meaning from that context. Advertising to doctors or engineers will sensibly avoid too much familiarity in addressing such readers but will use *you* and *your* freely in writing trade advertising addressed to retailers.

Much depends upon whether the conversational feeling is appropriate for the advertising you're writing. If it is, then informality is desirable—certainly that is the case for much consumer print advertisements and radio advertising.

Using *your* or *you* prominently doesn't necessarily guarantee anything. For example, 17 advertisements doing so were tested against 17 others that did not. Eight of the *you* advertisements were successful, but nine of the other ads were, too. No earthshaking conclusions may be drawn here, but mere inclusion of personal words is no certain route to success.

7. The benefit is not only rational.

In addition to the tangible benefits from using the product, there may be intangible benefits. This is especially so for many products where the physical differences between it and its competitor are not that great. The taste of two colas may be preferred by similar proportions of the population, but the meaning that Pepsi and Coke have to their loyal users varies significantly. How an ad conveys and reinforces that meaning, through its words and visuals, can be as important as some product's tangible benefits. Indeed the strongest benefits seem to be those that can be conveyed both rationally and emotionally.

What to Do to Get Attention, Create Desire, and Get Action When You Write Advertisements

For many years, advertising has been thought of as being part of a process that creates **A**wareness, builds **I**nterest, increases **D**esire, which leads to **A**ction. This is often called the AIDA model of advertising effect. More recently, many alternative views of advertising's role have been offered. Today, almost everyone recognizes that AIDA is a greatly oversimplified description of the process. Advertising effect is not necessarily linear, individual steps may be skipped entirely, and emotion-based response, which many feel lies outside of the AIDA model, can be more important than cognitive-based response that AIDA seems to prefer. Despite this evolution, AIDA remains a useful way to think about advertising performance and ad creation. Its different steps are relevant because all advertising should be successful on at least one of them. Importantly also, it is important to understand that the individual components of an ad do not influence each of the AIDA dimensions equally. The aspects of an ad that may go toward building awareness are not necessarily the same ones that go to building interest, desire, or action. So, in this context, we turn to AIDA as a means for helping us think about advertising construction.

In the AIDA model, attention and interest factors are closely related. First, you attract the attention of possible readers; then, you invite them to read the message by switching quickly from mere eye catching to interest building. Most frequently, attention and interest are developed through headline and illustration treatment. After that, the first paragraph of copy is simply a transition from the ideas conveyed by the headline and illustration, to additional support for the message.

ATTENTION

In order to tell anyone about something, you first must get attention at some level. This is true in personal conversation and in mass communication, including advertising. Advertising attention is meaningless, however, if it is not directed toward the product you are selling. Thus, it makes sense to properly draw the attention of the flip-and-run reader or the zipping-and-zapping television viewer to your message.

Advertisements that draw reader attention directly to a product benefit capture that interest more solidly than those that use attention-getting techniques merely for the sake of getting interest per se. Accordingly, a headline is more likely to attract attention if it promises a shortcut to a housewife scanning the shopping news. In a business publication, an illustration that visibly portrays a manufacturing cost cutter will be more likely to attract the attention of management-minded readers.

Importance of Attention Getting Varies with Audiences

Although attention getting has an effect on advertising results in all media, it is more important in some media than in others, especially in situations where you don't have an engaged audience.

Consider a highly engaging television show or magazine that holds you captive up to the moment the next commercial or ad appears. Your attention is more assured than in the situation where the nature of the media consumption process is to move on to the next show or magazine. In both cases, though, it may vanish quickly if the message does not offer an immediate promise of reward. Attention getting may be more important to the advertiser whose audience tends to be looking at advertising in that medium as more of an interruption than in a medium whose audiences more often view the advertising as being part of the viewing/reading/shopping experience. Media can help themselves by encouraging advertisers to run advertising that people like to look at.

Physical Elements and Devices Play a Part

Size, color, and unusual treatments attract attention, but a mere increase in size, the addition of color, or a switch to more unusual illustrations may not be enough. These techniques are successful in attracting attention only if they make the promise of a benefit more apparent to the audience. For example, we know from research that a dominant element such as a big illustration will increase attention. Still, to make this increased attention meaningful and/or cost-efficient, the illustration should be relevant to the product and/or interests of readers.

Time-tested devices can also capture attention. The winsome woman, the cute child, the darling dog all can capture attention in and of themselves. However, problems arise when attention is gained through devices like these and those devices are not integral to the product and the ad's message. Often, readers of such ads have little memory of what was being advertised.

Inevitably, we return to the principle that the content of communication is more vital to successful rapport with readers, viewers, and listeners than are the mechanical means of expression. It is what you say and show that provides the key to attention—the ideas, the suggestions of value, the promise of benefits to be received. Headlines and illustrations are simply tools for projecting that value.

INTEREST

Attracting interest in your advertising depends on both the tangible aspects, such as physical attributes, and the intangible ones, such as appealing ideas and emotions.

The advertisements whose physical attributes do the best job of translating attention into interest are the ones that are mechanically the easiest to read. Such advertisements are organized so logically that information is easy for the reader to grasp. Picture-caption advertisements illustrate the point, as do those set in easy-to-read typefaces and those from which all distracting elements have been cut.

Still, the value of a physically perfect advertisement will be small if the ideas are mundane. It is the ideas conveyed by the first elements of an advertisement that either build or preclude sufficient interest for the reader to want to dig deeper into the message.

You will find some advertisements that clearly demonstrate to the reader the benefit of finding out what is good about the products and how they will fit his or her needs. These advertisements are high in general interest, promise a story, suggest and answer to a universal problem, touch the reader's self-interest, look as if they contain specific information of great interest, and contain believable illustrations of the product in action.

DESIRE

Usually, more than anything else, the purpose of an advertisement is to increase the desire to own the product or use the service being advertised. As you will see from the researched advertisements in this book, most of the highly rated ones start immediately to build desire in headlines, illustrations, and introductory copy. Once again the importance of headline and illustration becomes apparent. One respected advertising agency head, in fact, told his creative people, "Put *everything* in the headline." To him, the reason for placing copy under a headline is to make the headline more important rather than draw attention to, or get results from, the copy itself. Few will agree that copy is *that* unimportant, arguing that it reinforces the ideas offered in the headlines and illustration. Copy, they say, reassures readers in many, and often new, ways that the product will benefit them to the point of convincing them to think about it in a more favorable way than they had before.

Results accrue from a composite of the effects created by headlines, illustrations, and copy. Yet the key almost always lies in the first impression conveyed in headlines and illustrations. If you can determine which advertisement the readers will feel offers the greatest benefit, you will have found the one that achieves the most results.

Specific, relevant, unique, believable, and wanted benefits are the touchstones of desire creation in successful advertising.

ACTION

Although immediate action is usually not expected from an advertisement, ultimate action and/or beliefs is always anticipated or hoped for. Because action is especially sought in mail order or direct response advertising, let us consider action in these terms.

In addition to direct sales, one measurement of effectiveness is the number of inquiries received. Inquiries come from people who presumably are good prospects. One way to spur inquiries is to use a coupon. Although couponed advertisements will generally outpull couponless ones, this is not always true—a couponless advertisement may have offered a benefit more relevant to the kind of people who were logical prospects for what was offered in the coupon.

You will also find instances in which smaller advertisements produced more inquiries than larger ones, and some cases in which larger advertisements were better at spurring action. A seeming contradiction? Not if you recognize that the mechanics of space size are not so important as the mental impact delivered by the idea quality of the content.

Moral: If you can use a larger space to create a picture of greater benefits, use it; but if you can not, use smaller advertisements with the possible added benefit of increasing reach or frequency. As the Newspaper Advertising Bureau has pointed out over and over again in its studies of copy effectiveness in newspapers, it is content that counts.

Another action question relating to mail order: Will inquiry returns drop if you charge for the sample or booklet offered? This question comes up when an advertiser offers something of value in general media. Such an advertiser usually wants to limit inquiries to logical prospects. Putting a nominal price on the offer is one way to make sure that inquiries will come from prospects only. Still, an advertiser hesitates to impose any block (even a small price) in the way of customer action.

In general, the results seem to vary more with what is offered than with the price of action. A charge for a worthwhile offer does not seem to reduce inquiries. Furthermore, in many cases of free offers, advertisers stress that there is no charge but neglect to put proper emphasis on the offer itself. It sometimes seems advisable to stress the value of the offer and play down the price or the fact that the offer is free.

All advertising is designed to produce sales in the long run, and only a small portion is aimed at direct orders obtained through advertising. As a rule, the copy researcher does not have actual sale results with which to demonstrate the effectiveness of advertisements. The researcher is most often looking at whether dispositions to use the product have been increased or attitudes about the brand have been enhanced. In mail order, the researcher has a solid measure of success—the number of orders obtained. This puts mail order in a class apart from other advertising.

SUMMARY

The most important element in producing sales results in an advertisement is the benefit it describes to the customer. It is the strong benefit that leads to more attention, interest, desire, and ultimately, action. Gimmicks, gadgets, and technique are distinctly subordinate to strong benefits; although poor technique can greatly impair strong messaging.

PACT Principles of Copy Testing

In 1982, 21[1] of what were then the major U.S. advertising agencies issued a public statement called PACT (Positioning Advertising Copy Testing). PACT represented their consensus on the fundamental principles underlying a good copy testing system. While many of these agencies have now merged, some with their names and identities lost, the principles still provide a solid foundation for understanding what constitutes effective advertising research and assessing copy research solutions.

Principle 1:
A good copy testing system provides measurements that are relevant to the objectives of the advertising.

Advertising is used (as are all marketing tools) to contribute to the achievement of marketing objectives-whether they be for a product, a service, or a corporation. The industry recognizes [as exemplified by the landmark "DAGMAR"[2] study of the Association of National Advertisers (ANA)] that the goal of advertising is to achieve specified objectives. It is further recognized that different advertisements can have a number of objectives, such as the following:

- Reinforcing current perceptions
- Encouraging trial of a product or service
- Encouraging new uses of a product or service
- Providing greater saliency for a brand or company name
- Changing perceptions and imagery
- Announcing new features and benefits

To be useful, a copy test for a given advertisement should be designed to provide an assessment of the advertisement's potential for achieving its stated objectives. Indeed, advertising objectives should be the first issue for discussion when a copy testing program is to be developed or a particular method is to be selected. In recognition of the fundamental importance of these objectives, every copy testing proposal and every report on results should begin with a clear statement of the advertising objectives.

Principle 2:
A good copy testing system is one that requires agreement about how the results will be used in *advance* of each specific test.

A primary purpose of copy testing is to *help* in deciding whether or not to run the advertising in the marketplace. A useful approach is to specify what are called "action standards" before the results are in. The following are some examples of possible action standards.

- Significantly improve perceptions of the brand as measured by _____.
- Achieve an attention level of at least _____% as measured by _____.
- Perform at least as well as (specify execution) as measured by _____.
- Produce negative responses of no higher than _____% as measured by _____.

The practice of specifying how the results will be used before they are in ensures that there is mutual

---

[1] The advertising agencies sponsoring PACT: N.W. Ayer, Inc.; Ted Bates Worldwide, Inc.; Batten, Barton, Durstine & Osborne, Inc.; Benton & Bowles, Inc.; Campbell-Mithun, Inc.; Dancer Fitzgerald Sample, Inc.; D'Arcy-MacManus & Masius, Inc.; Doyle Dane Bernbach, Inc.; Grey Advertising, Inc.; Kenyon & Eckhardt, Inc.; KM&G International, Inc.; Marschalk Campbell-Ewald Worldwide; Marsteller, Inc.; McCaffrey and McCall Inc.; McCann-Erickson, Inc.; Needham, Harper & Steers, Inc. Ogilvy & Mather, Inc.; SSC&B: Lintas Worldwide; J. Walter Thompson Company; Young & Rubicam.

[2] "Defining Advertising Goal for Measured Advertising Results," by the Association of National Advertisers, Copyright 1961.

understanding on the goals of the test and minimizes conflicting interpretations of the test once the results are in.

Moreover, prior discussion allows for the proper positioning of the action standards, since the copy test results are not, in most cases, the sole information used in deciding whether to use a particular advertisement. The results of any given copy test should be viewed in the context of a body of learning. Thus, prior discussion should take into account the following:

- How well the particular copy testing method used relates to the objectives of the advertising.

- The *range* of results that are realistically achievable for the advertising approach used and for the brand or company in question.

- The entire search context (including other types of studies) for the tested ad and for similar ads.

A discussion of these issues prior to initiating a copy test provides benefits for both the advertisers and the agency. It minimizes the risks inherent in using copy test results in a mechanistic way, isolated from other learning. It maximizes the opportunity to draw upon learning and seasoned judgment of the advertiser and the agency as both parties reach for the best possible advertising.

Principle 3:
A good copy testing system provides *multiple* measurements, because single measurements are generally inadequate to assess the performance of an advertisement.

With the exception of corporate advocacy advertising, it is commonly believed that the ultimate measurement by which advertising should be judged is its *contribution* to sales. But the complexity of the marketing process and the constraints of time and money usually preclude rigorous testing—that is, testing that can separate the effects of advertising from the many other factors that influence sales and thereby provide an estimate of the sales contribution of a given advertisement prior to a national launch. Nor is there any universally accepted single measurement that can serve as a surrogate for sales.

Moreover, the communication process is complex. To understand this process, and to learn from each successive test, it is necessary to use multiple measures-measures that reflect the multifaceted nature of communications. However, the inclusion of multiple measures should not imply that all measures have equal weight in evaluating the advertising. As noted

previously, in advance of each test, agreement should be reached as to the relative importance of the various measurements in judging the acceptability of the tested execution.

Principle 4:
A good copy testing system is based on a model of human response to communications—the *reception* of a stimulus, the comprehension of the stimulus, and the *response* to the stimulus.

PACT agencies view advertising as performing on several levels. To succeed, an advertisement must have an effect:

- On the "eye," on the "ear": *It must be received* (RECEPTION)

- On the "mind": *It must be understood* (COMPREHENSION)

- On the "heart": *It must make an impression* (RESPONSE)

It therefore follows that a good copy testing system should answer a number of questions. Listed below are examples of the kinds of questions relevant to these communications issues. The order of the listing does not relate to priority of importance. As discussed in the preceding principles, priorities will vary depending on the objectives of the specific advertising being tested.

Reception
— Did the advertising "get through"?
— Did it catch the consumer's attention?
— Was it remembered?
— Did it catch the consumer's eye? The consumer's ear?

Comprehension
— Was the advertising understood?
— Did the consumer "get" the message?
— Was the message identified with the brand?
— Was anything confusing or unclear?

Response
— Did the consumer accept the proposition?
— Did the advertising affect attitudes toward the brand?
— Did the consumer think or "feel" differently about the brand after exposure?

— Did the advertising affect perceptions of the brand?

— Did the advertising alter perceptions of the set of competing brands?

— Did the consumer respond to direct action appeals?

Another area of response measurements relates to executional elements. PACT agencies agree that it is useful to obtain responses to these elements of an advertisement.

Executional Diagnostics: Questioning about consumers' reactions to the advertising execution (e.g., perceived differentiation from other advertising, reactions to music, to key phrases, to presenters or characters, to story elements, etc.) can provide insight about the strengths and weaknesses of the advertising and why it performed as it did.

PACT agencies use different measures to address the issues in these four areas. However, they are all based on the same fundamental understanding of the communication process.

Principle 5:
A good copy testing system allows for consideration of whether the advertising stimulus should be exposed more than once.

Extensive experimentation in the field of communications and learning has demonstrated that learning of test material is far higher after two exposures than after one—and that subsequent exposures do not yield as large an increase as that between the first and second exposure.

In light of the experimental work, PACT agencies share the view that the issue of single versus multiple exposures should be carefully considered in each test situation. There are situations in which a single exposure would be sufficient-given the objectives of the advertising and the nature of the test methodology. There are other situations where a single exposure could be inadequate—particularly high-risk situations, subtle or complex communications, and questioning about executional diagnostics.

Principle 6:
A good copy testing system recognizes that the more finished a piece of copy is, the more soundly it can be evaluated and requires, as a minimum, that alternative executions be tested in the same degree of finish.

Experience has shown that test results can often vary depending on the degree of finish of the test

executions. Thus, careful judgment should be used in considering the importance of what may be lost in a less-than-finished version. Sometimes this loss may be consequential; sometimes it may be critical.

The judgment of the advertising creators should be given great weight as to the degree of finish required to represent the finished advertisement for test purposes. If there is a reason to believe that alternative executions would be unequally penalized in the pre-production form, then it is generally advisable to test them in a more finished form. If alternative executions are tested in different stages of finish within the same test, then it is impossible to ensure that the results are not biased due to the varying degrees of finish.

Principle 7:
A good copy testing system provides controls to avoid the biasing effects of exposure context.

Extensive work in the field of communications and learning has demonstrated that the perception of and response to a stimulus is affected by the context in which the stimulus is presented and received.

In the case of advertising, it has been demonstrated, for example, that recall of the same commercial can vary depending on a number of conditions such as whether exposure to the commercial:

- Is off-air versus on-air
- Is in a cluttered reel of commercials versus a program context
- Is in one specific program context versus another specific program context

Thus, PACT agencies share the view that it is imperative to control the biasing effects of variable exposure contexts.

Principle 8:
A good copy testing system is one that takes into account basic considerations of sample definition.

- The testing should be conducted among a sample of the target audience for the advertised product. Limiting testing to the general population without provision for separate analysis of the target audience can be misleading.
- The sample should be representative of the target audience. To the degree that the sample drawn does not represent the target audience, the users of the research should be informed about the possible effects of the lack of representativeness on the interpretation of test results.

- The sample should take into account any geographical differences if they are critical to the assessment of the performance of a brand or service.
- The sample should be of sufficient size to allow a decision based on the obtained data to be made with confidence.

Principle 9:
A good copy testing system is one that can demonstrate reliability and validity.

To provide results that can be used with confidence, a copy testing system should be:

- *Reliable.* It should yield the same results each time that the advertising is tested. If, for example, a test of multiple executions does not yield the same rank order of performance on the test/retest, the test is not reliable and should not be used to judge the performance of commercials. Tests in which external variables are not held constant will probably yield unreliable results.

- *Valid.* It should provide results that are relevant to marketplace performance. PACT agencies recognize that demonstration of validity is a major and costly undertaking requiring industry-wide participation. While some evidence of predictive validity is available, many systems are in use for which no evidence of validity is provided. We encourage the cooperation of advertisers and agencies in pursuit of this critical need.

Interviews with Experts: Answers to Common and Important Questions about Advertising

This section presents interviews with some leading advertising authorities. They discuss candidly and informally various aspects of print advertising, with special emphasis on creative matters.

Also included is an interview with George Gallup, which appeared in the previous editions of *Which Ad Pulled Best?* It is repeated largely as it was originally given, although some dated material has been deleted. Because it provides valuable insights by one of the great authorities in communication, it has been included again. Furthermore, the principles expressed by Dr. Gallup are presciently timeless in their application.

In some instances the questions asked of the experts are similar. It is interesting and valuable to see how different respondents answer the same questions and—in so many instances—to see how closely they agree on the basic principles of advertising and advertising creativity.

George Gallup
GALLUP & ROBINSON, INC.

Q: In the course of the years, have you found much change in the way advertising works-in the kind of advertising that works best?

A: No, I wouldn't say so. The copywriters change. But the kind of copy that has always worked still works. The problem is not so much one of finding out what new appeals work better today as it is of educating the new people who are coming along all the time in the basic principles of advertising. And, as a matter of fact, the old-timers seem to need reminding every now and then on the basics. We have to keep re-proving old truths in terms of new products and new markets.

Q: In the course of your experience with advertisers— and particularly with their advertising agencies—has any particular weak spot in the whole process of presenting sales ideas in advertising struck you as most needing correction?

A: Well, I suppose there are a lot of weak spots. I'd say that the most greatly overlooked opportunity is that of advertising products. We find an awful lot of advertisers seem to be afraid to tell people about their products. But the public is very interested in products. They want to know all about these products that they can buy.

We have too much advertising that starts out talking about something else that is presumably of great interest to prospective customers and then, after an involved transition, gets around to admitting that something's for sale. Actually, people read ads because they want to know what's for sale.

Q: You say that people want to know about prices and about what's new in products and about what products will do. Would you say that any one of these elements is most important?

A: No, because it depends on the product, on competition in the field, and on the different levels of different kinds of merchandise—and on a lot of other things. But I would say that there's an awful lot more news about products than many advertisers recognize. The opportunity is there for copy people to search out newsy things about products. A new price is in itself news. A new product is news. A new ingredient is news. A way of making a product stronger is news. There are a million and one things about products that relate to the benefits to be secured from buying them that are news. It's up to the copy people to wring this information out of the production people who know the facts but who don't realize their (the fact's) value to advertising.

Q: Is it the words, then, that are used in advertising copy that make the difference? Does the phraseology?

A: No, not words or phrases, but *ideas*. That's what distinguishes, perhaps more than anything else, the advertising that penetrates from that which does not get under the skin of the people who see or read or hear it. The important thing is to present ideas forcefully. Words and images are the vehicles, of course, for all expression. But they are not good unless they mean something worthwhile to the folks on the receiving end.

Q: Could you be a little more specific in what you mean by the forceful presentation of ideas?

A: This is the big difference between advertisements—it's not one of using magic words. Boast copy is no good, no matter how many so-called magic words are strewn all the way through it. Proof copy, on the other hand—that is, believable proof copy—is the kind of thing that sticks with people. Demonstrations always have been effective. The before-and-afters are magic, not because of the words used or the size of the pictures so much as because of the magic in the idea, the proof of value.

One of the most interesting things about this whole question is that the kind of advertising that is most effective is the kind that is approved by the general public. The advertisements that cause complaints by the public are those that miss the boat—the boastful advertisements, the ones with the lack of proof, the ones that are cluttered up with "adiness" instead of performing the service for which advertising is ideally suited: telling people about the true benefits of merchandise.

Q: How about the physical appearance of advertisements? Is there any general criterion that separates the good from the bad advertising in this respect?

A: I guess the most generally applicable rule of thumb would be to separate advertisements into those with gimmicks and those without. The gimmicky advertisements usually don't work. Gimmicks tend to get in the way of idea expression. By this I mean all kinds of gimmicks: trick headlines, color just for the

sake of adding something extra, unusual typography, excessive use of tint block, copy patches that mutilate a main illustration, crazy pictures that have no relation to the product being sold. These things create "adiness"; they take away from the clear expression of the many things about products that are of very great interest to the public.

Q: Along these lines, it seems as though quite a lot of advertisers believe that they have to entertain as they sell. Aren't many of these gimmicks put in for entertainment value of a sort?

A: I suppose many of the gimmicks are put in for entertainment value. But the thing is that people don't read advertisements to be entertained so much as to learn something about the products. It all comes back to the lack of appreciation of the interest of the public in merchandise—not just plain old merchandise, but new merchandise, new things about merchandise, new ways to use merchandise. There's plenty of entertainment value of a sort in the products, provided the copy writer is smart enough to find it and present it in a forthright and interesting manner.

Q: Do you find that in a medium such as TV (technologically so far removed from, say, magazine advertising) the kind of copy approach that is most effective is very different from those that you have found resultful in other media?

A: No, not really. In television there is a difference that results from having a captive audience to start with. You can jump right into the selling copy without having to snag attention first. The attention is there, so you go directly into the interest and desire-building process. Tricky wind-ups and abstruse lead-ins are usually a waste of valuable time in TV commercials. Additionally, in television you have the added dimensions of sound and motion to help. But aside from these considerations, the basics of persuasion are the same.

Q: How long has Gallup & Robinson been testing TV commercials?

A: We have been operating a television service—serving regular clients in this respect—since November of 1951. For about two years before that time, we were developing the research methods we use.

Q: Could you describe in very general terms what those methods are?

A: Very briefly, our methods of judging TV impact are of the same nature as those we apply in studying the impact of magazine advertisements. We concern ourselves with the thoughts and feelings a person has when an advertiser tries to register a sales message with him or her. We are looking at how well the advertising succeeds in making an impression and doing it in a persuasive fashion.

Q: Do you find much difference in the impact made by different TV commercials?

A: Oh, yes—a tremendous amount of difference. On average we experience a more than six-to-one difference in the levels of recall and persuasion. And then, of course, we get wide range in the playback of the selling messages and in the conviction, believability, and involvement that become apparent. You've got to keep in mind that the advertiser is paying the same amount of money to reach each of these levels of effectiveness.

Q: How did the G&R Impact methodology evolve?

A: At Young & Rubicam, we gained important insights about the methodology itself. While readership findings proved to be extremely helpful in reaching a larger audience with the advertiser's message, they did not provide all the information that was needed to produce effective advertising. The findings did not, for example, reveal how many of those who had seen or read given advertisements registered on the copy message or, for that matter, on the brand name. Nor did they shed light on the buying urge created by the copy.

To bridge this gap, a series of experiments was undertaken during the late 1930s and the early 1940s. This experimentation resulted in the development of the impact method, which sought to move beyond reading and noting data and to measure such factors as registration of brand name and such qualitative parameters as idea communication and urge to buy. The new method could be used not only with print but with broadcast advertising as well. The first test of the method was a stripped-down copy of the April 16, 1945, issue of *Life* magazine with test ads "tipped-in." While we were working on these experiments at Young & Rubicam between 1945 and 1947, Dr. Claude Robinson, who founded Opinion Research Corporation (ORC), was conducting similar studies with a magazine called *Space*.

This experimentation eventually led to the impact method, which was fully in place by 1945. In 1947 I left Y&R to join Claude Robinson in a new venture called Gallup & Robinson to carry on research in advertising.

Q: As you look back over your career in research, would you give us your impression of the various trends or changes that have occurred?

A: There have been many, many schools, one succeeding the other, in the history of copy research, when everybody ran this way and then ran that way. Of course, this is true in every field; one school succeeds another. But I think there's a trend back to the basics—not only in the United States, but all around the world. The first job of advertising is to get seen and read and then to change people's attitudes.

Q: How would that translate itself in terms of either research techniques or research philosophies?

A: I don't think it would change the philosophies. The techniques need to be redefined and improved. This whole problem of isolating and weighing the influence of advertising on a sale is a very sticky problem and always has been. You're trying to isolate advertising and its influence; you're trying to sort it out from a hundred other identifiable factors. I think it can be done, and it's amazing to me that more people aren't studying from year to year the advertising that is succeeding and what the factors are that are common to it as opposed to the advertising that demonstrably isn't succeeding.

Q: How should an advertiser evaluate how effective an advertising campaign is?

A: Almost every campaign, to begin with, has specific objectives. The whole process of advertising is designing a strategy that will create a sale. You can find out if the strategy is working. Are you changing people's minds about this particular fact about the product? You can measure that. All advertisers, even if they spend only a few thousand dollars, should demand some kind of evidence of the effectiveness of their advertising. And I am shocked, really, that sometimes advertisers spend millions of dollars without demanding that kind of evidence.

Q: Of course, there are various schools of copy testing.

A: And every school claims to be "the" school. But I think that the most useful, truthful way of thinking of copy testing is to regard all of the methods as useful and serving a given purpose. There isn't any method that will cover the waterfront. This is the mistake all schools of thought make. They believe if they find a cure for headache it will also cure flat feet; but one must know the limitations of each method. Being a good copy researcher is a matter of knowing exactly what each method will do, what its strengths are, and what its limitations are, and not trying to come to some overall conclusion that if it's good in this area it has to be great.

Q: What would you say is the major issue in survey research?

A: Sampling obviously has to be number one. In the first part of this century, it was bad sampling that made the *Literary Digest* come up with the most inaccurate poll results in history, an error of 19 percentage points on a presidential election. They were sampling by mail and sampling people who had telephones and automobiles, which at that time was relatively atypical. We changed that to quota sampling up to 1948. Then our mistake, our election of Tom Dewey instead of Truman in 1948, was due largely to timing factors. At that point in history, we had to stop about 10 days to two weeks before the election. After 1948 we had to invent ways of polling up through Saturday noon before election, because there are significant changes in those last few days. Now we can be accurate to tenths of percentage points.

David Apicella
CO-CREATIVE CHIEF OGILVY AND MATHER

Q: What's a good working definition of advertising?

A: Advertising is communication that tries to persuade consumers to do something—buy, act, vote, whatever—depending on what is being advertised. It certainly also creates awareness. It's some kind of awareness and persuasion combination.

Q: Why do people look at advertising if that's all it does?

A: Because it can be pretty entertaining. One of the things that advertisers have to do to get people to notice them is to entertain. People say they don't like advertising, but I don't believe that; I think they just don't like boring advertising. Good advertising is highly popular. Good advertising is just as interesting as the show editorial content in which it appears.

Q: When you approve advertising, how do you judge whether it's good or not?

A: The first thing I look for is, is it on strategy? Is it saying the thing that we have decided we need to say? The second thing I look at is, are we doing it in a fresh, compelling, interesting way so that the average consumer, who has neither my experience nor interest, will they pay attention to it?

Q: Can you share with us an example or case history that shows the power of advertising to work?

A: Dove's "The Campaign for Real Beauty" is a great example about what advertising does when it operates at its absolute best. What the campaign does is tap into a cultural truth or phenomenon, which is that women don't like to be spoken to the way they were spoken to by the beauty industry. It made them feel insecure and inferior and all sorts of things. By doing advertising at a higher level, and here it doesn't even talk about products, it talks about this larger beauty issue, and people do run out and buy the products.

Q: Why do advertisers use print?

A: Well, they do so less frequently than they used to. Print media are going through some seismic changes. It depends on the market. When I say that, I'm really speaking about the most sophisticated media markets with the most advanced technologies one can get. When you go to other parts of the world, Third World countries in particular, there is still far more print than there is television. Traditionally, people used television when they could afford it for awareness—in 30 seconds you can only communicate so much and you can only really just pique people's interest. They use print to fill in the holes in reach and go into greater detail about why someone should do whatever it is the advertiser hopes they will do.

Q: Are there certain stories that are better told in print?

A: Any kind of long copy story. On a newspaper page, you can run a lot of words. You can tell quite a long story. You could never do anything comparable to that with television.

Q: Is "long copy" still a viable form of print advertising?

A: No, probably not so much, sadly. It is ironic because David Ogilvy was a great proponent of "long copy." Our agency, probably as much as another, was built on that idea. It seems to be one of the styles that is going away in a major way. Every once in a while you still see well-executed long-copy creative. Some of our colleagues in Asia are making good use of it. If it is well done, people are interested in it, but there is less of it in use today.

Q: When you look at a print ad, what would you look at to judge whether it will be effective or not?

A: It's mainly about the headline and the visual. You need a clever headline and/or a striking visual to get people's interest.

Q: When you start in an agency, what media do you typically start in?

A: It used to be that print was the thing you did before you did anything else. Print ads used to be the entry level way into our copywriter jobs. You had to be able to be clever on print just to get in the door. When I started here on the TWA account, I was hired as a copywriter. It was a high-churn retail account where you had new ads twice a week in 56 cities. I was part of a room full of 23 year-olds who didn't know any better and would just sit there and crank these things out. There was a week, early in my career, where I wrote 56 ads in one week! Mostly you would write a template and the price and other detail information might change by city. The ads might have a companion piece in radio. You did that for years before anyone would let you near a television commercial which was, back then, the "Holy Grail" of advertising. It still is the thing. Some broadcast stuff you can watch is still kind of the prize, even though it may take place on YouTube these days.

Q: How are print ads created today?

A: We start with the strategy and the problem that needs to be solved. There's not a button that you push or a process that you could point to that would be the definitive way you do that. We sit in teams still for the most part. The traditional combination is writer/art director and it's still kind of that, but they might have slightly different designations because there are interactive people who are creating things for the Web. People still probably either have a writer bias or an art bias, though increasingly everybody has to do everything. Then, we sit together in a room with a strategy, with the actual strategy document that is created by an account planner. The account person tends to the relationship with the client. The creative team creates the work. The planner divines the strategy from the conversations with all parties, keeping sense of what the customer's need might be, and that's usually written in the strategy. So, you have this document on your desk that basically is a problem to be solved and you sit with a partner. Now they have a term that didn't exist when I started, which is to "concept." So we "concept" and come up with an idea or several ideas, a couple of headlines or a headline, and you put it all together on a page and show it to your boss or an associate. They say, "Great" or "Go back and do it again."

Q: Do you typically produce more than one alternative to take to a client?

A: Yes, clients like to see a range of things. The range will often be from what we call "close ins," so that's the most expected thing, which will usually be the safest thing, the least provocative or edgy, to something that pushes things and may push the client a bit. Often times, creative guys want the edgy things because they're usually the most creative. It's not necessarily the best and not always right, but we always want to go out there a little bit to keep things moving forward.

Q: Is the process similar if it's television?

A: If there's a problem, there's some type of official document that represents the problem. If there's a problem to be solved, it's the creative people's job to solve it in whatever medium is appropriate and that's the big change. When I started I might say, "This needs a 60-second television commercial around the Super Bowl." But, nowadays it might be, "This needs a viral thing that goes on YouTube." More to the point and importantly, there is often a confluence. This has been led by some of the smaller, hipper agencies. The big agencies, like Ogilvy, are in the process of adapting and changing some of the ways they do things to stay current. Increasingly there are almost no clients now that don't talk about, "What's the media-neutral solution? Here's my problem. I don't care where and how it runs, just as long as it does the thing I need it to do." That's a profound change.

Q: *So, by that you mean it's not thought of as "I need a television commercial" or "let's do something for print"?*

A: In fact, I would go further than that, and this is maybe a trend: there's almost a bias against media-specific solutions, especially television commercials. If you go in with just a television commercial these days, many clients will say, "Why didn't you think more broadly about the options out there." So, today, we tend to bring in more holistic things. This is particularly the case, if you are advertising to younger people, and advertisers for the most part are almost always speaking to younger audiences unless they're in a luxury business.

Q: *What kind of people are you hiring to help push in that direction? And how has that changed?*

A: That's interesting too. Well, you hire people these days that come out of ad schools. The ad schools are producing graduates who have exactly what I'm talking about. They solve the problem from scratch regardless of media and are adept in all the disciplines. They don't even think that this is a television or a print ad. They'll just come up with an idea and then they will sort of look at the idea and determine or, at least, recommend the best place for it to go.

Q: *For someone thinking about getting into the creative side of the advertising business, would you recommend that they go to an ad school rather than a liberal arts or business college?*

A: Ad school is usually after college. You usually get your degree, and, if you're interested, then you go to one of these programs. I would say, though, that it is the ad schools that are producing the creative talent, not the business schools. The ad schools are preparing creative people to think about problems in this kind of new world, which is natural to them because they

grew up on the Internet. Ad schools are usually one or two years long and they help you put together a portfolio. Then you need to get a job as a creative person in an advertising agency or a media company. Increasingly, media companies are treading in the same space that advertising agencies historically have, which is to say that they are creating content and therefore hiring or using creative people. I can't tell you the 10 things you need to be a creative person in an ad agency, but I can tell you that every good creative person is curious about the world and pretty much all things in it. Because of that, it doesn't really matter what your background is. These days you need some expertise in digital applications, but to today's young people that comes naturally. My own personal case had me going to law school before I got into advertising, which is certainly not the traditional path. Somewhere along the way, in the course of that, I found myself more interested in the idea of advertising. When in law school, I had gotten into analyzing commercials on television. I don't know why. I would see how they structured it and I was fascinated by the logic of the argument that they constructed to try and get me to use their product. With that kind of interest and curiosity, you can be doing about anything and there will be a place for you in advertising if you're good at it.

Q: *When the student presents his or her portfolio, is that something he or she has created themselves?*

A: Yes, they create it, usually with a partner because we still pair people up. And again, there is a writer/art bias usually, but they both can do everything. You get out of the school with what we call a book. The schools are pretty aggressive about building relationships with key people in the agencies. Most of the big agencies have a creative recruiter. It's in the agencies' interest to find the best young talent and we kind of do that together. The schools seek us out and we seek them out and we do a lot of portfolio reviews. The schools will have portfolio weekends and they will invite people from all the agencies to come down and look. So once a student is in this system, they will get their fair shot.

Q: *Does personality enter into it?*

A: It does. I do think, though, that a lot of successful creative people are shy. Somehow you develop some of your abilities sitting around dark corners and musing. Having said that, no doubt in any discipline of advertising the people with the bigger personalities tend to get to the top of the heap. It really is a people business and you have to interact with others. If you are a creative person you have to sell your idea to a pretty long list of people including, ultimately, the client. You will have to use your own personal charms and arguments to persuade them to buy your ad. Also there are many other big personalities around and you can get steamrolled.

Q: In the new media, is that changing the pairing-up idea?

A: It doesn't seem to be. Some people are capable of executing an idea alone, but they're still going to be better off if they can work with someone to get the idea, or somebody who is going to write the software and do the technical things. The schools use pairs; we use pairs. It helps when you're a creative person to have another point of view. It's a little less scary and usually it enhances the idea. The traditional teams are two, but when I worked with Jerry Seinfeld on American Express, we used the model of his show. Instead of just having the writer/art director team or a couple writer/art director teams, we had a group of people who functioned much like the show's writers. We had five people to solve the problem because the end product would be better when five points of view are thrown at it.

Q: Some people talk about rational advertising and emotional advertising. Is that a distinction that makes sense to you?

A: You need both! An ad has to be on strategy and that's usually the rational part. It has to have some logic to it. And then you need the emotional part because that's the way human beings interact, with some type of emotional bond to everything—people, ads, products.

Q: So, the strictly rational type of appeal is not enough?

A: It depends on the product. You may need to be more rational in your ad if you have a thing that needs to be demonstrated or explained, but you still have to do it in a way that appeals to people on an emotional level. It still has to make you smile or laugh or feel tingly or whatever, even if they're just selling you a car. Buying a car is a good example. It's a perfect combination. It's highly rational and it's thoroughly emotional.

Q: Companies have some highly structured audience segments that they want to talk to. When you are creating advertising, are you creating it for those specific segments?

A: Yes, we almost never position a product or do an ad for absolutely everyone. Sometimes we will even pick our creative team based on the segment of interest. The way we operate, though, no one does anything alone here. There's a series of supervisors all along the way, so that we make sure that the end product checks all the boxes—all the rational/emotional boxes, on strategy, etc.

Q: How do you give feedback to a creative team?

A: It's always intuitive. I mean, I never knew it, you just learn by doing. Anybody who advances through the creative department gets to the point where, with his or her own experience, the numbers of times they've critiqued stuff, you're right more often than you're wrong. I push back when things are off in tone and maybe making the point that we want to make, but they're making it in a way that's inappropriate for the brand. "Off brand" we'll call it. A brand has its own sort of values and standards. That's kind of rule number one, you have to be true to the brand.

Q: Please talk about how you know when a campaign has become stale and it is time to move on.

A: Generally speaking, agencies and clients tire of the advertising faster and sooner than the consumers do because we're looking at it and thinking about it all day, every day. I know there isn't that level of interest out there in the real world. So, we will likely want to pull the plug on a campaign before a consumer will feel it should be done. But, sometimes the world changes, and the thing about advertising is that it has to be relevant. I mean that in a cultural way. You have to be true to what's of interest at the moment and, because our culture is always evolving and changing, your work can become out of step. I've personally been part of a couple of campaigns that have had really long lives. One is the Hershey's Kisses campaign with the little Hershey's Kisses jumping or dancing around on the white space that ran for 15 years. It could probably run today; it only changed when we stopped having a relationship with the Hershey Company. Sometimes you hit on one that is timeless; rarely does that happen, but every once in a while it does. Usually things change every couple of years because the world changes or the product has some news that needs to be communicated and therefore deserves a new plug.

Q: Is there one myth about advertising that you would like to dispel?

A: There are no subliminal messages.

Q: In your view, what kind of person should be attracted to working in advertising?

A: People who are curious about life and care about people. Because we are communicating and trying to get into the hearts and minds of people, you have to care about the world. You have to be interested in everything and like a good laugh. Advertising is a lot of fun and it's changing rapidly as the world changes, as technology changes the world. Advertising and communications businesses are at the leading edge of that. It's a very different life than crunching numbers on Wall Street. Everything about the communications business is creative, so if you have a creative interest or inclination, it's worth thinking about. Life in an advertising agency, particularly in the creative department, is hard work, long hours, and a lot of fun. And that's not so bad.

Q: Bill Bernbach said that he felt that creative was so important that one creative product could have a factor of 10 times the power of another or maybe even more. Is creative today that important in terms of how successful advertising is?

A: It's the whole thing. As I said in the beginning, people don't hate advertising, they hate bad advertising. Great advertising is, as you see on the Super Bowl, as popular as the game itself. So, it's yes. As the price of entry, you have to be good, but the great ones, as the great Bill Bernbach said, will lift like a million elephants. It's amazing what a great ad can do.

Interview with Christopher Becker
CHAIRMAN AND CHIEF CREATIVE OFFICER
DRAFTFCB NEW YORK

Q: What is a good definition of advertising?

A: We used to define advertising as a tool, as an execution. Now advertising has become an experience.

So it's a totally different way to define what good advertising is. If we think in terms of specific executions, it's easy to explain what a good print ad is, what a good TV ad is, what a great interactive site is. But the definition of execution has changed, and is changing, because the business has changed. The business has changed because the consumer has changed. Consumers are digesting advertising in different ways. Good advertising engages, embraces, and creates an experience. Advertising has become a duality—communication flowing not just from the advertiser to the audience, but back and forth between the two.

Q: How do you differentiate advertising from entertainment?

A: We're living in a world of entertainment. Brilliant work is executed in a way that entertains. If not, it's boring. Boring is probably the worst word you can find in the advertising world.

Q: Why do people look at advertising?

A: Basically because sometimes advertising touches something in our souls and at least in our thinking that is relevant to us. Relevance is the word. Sometimes you listen to someone and you can simply laugh or respect that person and really be engaged by the message. Brand links are very important. If you build a brand that everybody knows, like Apple, for example; whatever Apple has to say you listen. And from a message point of view, a well-crafted advertisement always entertains.

Q: How do you judge whether or not an advertisement is effective?

A: A lot of it has to do with visceral reaction based on experience. If you ask me why I had this reaction at that moment, that instant when I saw the idea it's based on my judgment. Good advertising is a great message that works. Advertising should be simple, loud, and expansive. If any of those three is lacking, probably it's not as good as it should be.

Q: Why do advertisers use print?

A: When you have the jewel of a print ad in front of you, you have the opportunity for a deep interaction between the brand and the consumer. It's a difficult challenge, though, because you have to find a way that makes someone spend more than two seconds on your ad. Print is changing a bit. In the past it was a destination. Now print is becoming more of a springboard to something else. In the past, when you read it, you get everything, including many of the facts. Now, it gets you to go to the Internet. People also do print because it's extremely important to have an icon that you own. An icon is very difficult to own through film, but it is very easy to own through print. From a creative's point of view, print is probably one of the few pieces of advertising where you have entire control. From the typeface to the product shoot to the layout, any detail in a print ad can be controlled. You definitely have the entire process in your hands, which is a very nice feeling for a creative person. TV has to be handed over to the director, who interprets what you're doing. Print is something you can touch.

Q: Print used to be a strong number two to television. Is that changing and, if so, how?

A: That's a question more about the media than print by itself. What's going to happen with TV, radio, newspapers, magazines, and online in the future? Some people say TV is going to be what disappears. I don't think that's true. It's not all going to disappear. Maybe everything is going to end up on the computer, but the needs and the skills to fulfill those needs are going to be the same. Whatever one is trying to accomplish with a print ad is going to need to be accomplished somewhere else. We are living in a world of changing media consumption. But quality will survive and one would expect there would be room for well-crafted magazines that you respect and have great editorial and advertising in them.

Q: Does online advertising communicate as well emotionally as print ads? Does the tactile experience of a print ad or the physicality of it make a difference in terms of how you connect with your audience?

A: I have always felt that print for a consumer is the most intimate approach to advertising; more so than anything else. You almost feel that some ads are speaking to you, especially when they touch your sense of design. High-end advertising, particularly, has a depth that no other medium can offer. Print can connect at a deeper level. It's the only medium that allows you the ability to tear the page out of the magazine, put it in front of you, and start dreaming. You can't do that with a TV ad. You can't do that with an outdoor billboard. You can't even do that with online. You can do it with a print ad.

Q: How do you create a print ad at your agency?

A: From a creative point of view, each art director has his own technique. I was taught to create by using a very small space. You have to be very clear how you express yourself in the little space. You learn how to handle spaces, how to handle white. You use a copywriter and an art director to create the piece. Maybe it's just a word that leads you to the idea. In the past we only had copywriters and art directors. Now, sometimes it's two art directors creating one ad or sometimes you have two copywriters creating one ad, which is very interesting. And then you have the working design. Once you have the idea, we go to the computer. My suggestion to people who design print is that they have to know how to tell the computer what they want. That's coming from the creative point of view and what I recommend. Later on you go through the processes of the agency. We have a great art buying department so you have the best photographers, in case you need a photographer. If you need to illustrate, you can find an illustrator. You are basically open to the entire world and the best people. We're very respectful with print.

Q: Often advertisers talk about segmenting the audience different ways according to demographics, psychographics, and the like. How much do audience segmentation issues enter into how you think about creating an ad?

A: It's key. It's absolutely key, especially in these times where people are empowered. People build their own personality bubbles. It should be very clear what kind of people we are talking to. Trends and different kinds of esthetics and fashions can exert huge influences. You need to clearly identify those people and use language and symbols that are going to touch their souls. If you want to touch a soul you have to know the soul before you touch it.

Q: How do you find that out?

A: We have a great process. What we basically do is expose ourselves to the "smart wall." The smart wall is organic data. It's a wall of computer screens. Each screen represents a demographic, location, trend, cycle, graphics, or even film with those people that we have in focus groups so you can see that. You can pull them out. Basically what you do is feed the computer with what you need and then screens will tell you who they are and what they do, how they behave, what they drink, how they eat, how they sleep. If you had a Product X and a defined market for that, you can find who the person is here. Each screen has a headline idea and the headlines bring to life what each screen is. It gives us support for our work, and you can easily walk out of the room and create. Sometimes, people digest the wall and they give you a speech in a very organic and demographic way about where the target people live, what they do, and how they behave. You see results in real time, which is extremely interesting. For a creative, it facilitates my life by diminishing risk and elevating creative freedom.

Q: How do you know when a campaign becomes stale?

A: It depends on what goal you had. If the goal is sales, that's very easy. It's not selling anymore. So you have to react or you have to build or refresh or simply you realize that what you came up with is not solid enough to be built on so you have to come up with something new. But you can't merely be reactive. Refreshing is key and you have to do it constantly. Once you get stale, you are in trouble and you run the risk that you will lose the account. We are constantly rethinking what we're doing; it has to come from us. It shouldn't have to come from the market. If we wait until the market tells us it's stale, we are in trouble because by the time the market lets you know, you've already been in it for a year.

Q: What should young people do to prepare themselves for their first job in the agency world?

A: I look for people who have traveled a lot. That would be experiencing other cultures. Creatives create something they have experienced, so I like the people who have traveled a lot and been exposed to different cultures, different countries, and different ways of living, be it drinking tea or coffee, how they eat or how they behave. You have to be an expert at behavior and you can only be that by seeing it. That's number one. Number two is even more important in these times where everything is so connected. In the past when you needed a specific art director, you hired an art director. You went through the book and you went through the skills and you hired the skill-set you were looking for. Now, I'm looking for total thinkers: people who don't distinguish between print, TV, outdoor, and alternative media or artificial media and people who understand that this world is eclectic and it's not

pigeonholed anymore. Even if later on their skills are closer to print or TV, we'll find out, but overall their approach should be open—extremely open. And then we go from there.

Q: Must they have a portfolio?

A: Yes, I'm very bad with that because I don't look at portfolios. I judge the person, but their portfolios have been screened by the time they get to me. And they have often gone to the advertising schools. We have hired some who have never been to any of the schools or do not have a portfolio. We have so many spaces at the agency where someone can make an impact on what content should be, on the cell phone or anything, that I really don't mind where that person is coming from, unless I have a certain need for a certain client and I'm looking for a specific person. But if not, I am open to any great talent that senses how communication should work, with travel, again, being key.

Q: Do you have any feelings about the type of personality that is successful in today's agency environment?

A: People need to be hungry for experience. We do these creative rumbles that bring people in from all over the world to create a campaign for a specific brand. Most of the people don't know each other and we see how they react in that environment. You have people in a room who don't say a word for three days. And the last day they come up and they have five campaigns. There are people who don't stop talking for the entire time and that's how they work. How a person is, is often just his or her artistic approach to things. But if they are not hungry, they shouldn't come to this business because they are going to suffer too much. They should love the creation process.

Q: Is there anything you wish you knew when you began your career?

A: Learn earlier to believe in yourself. That is more important than trying to analyze what's in the books. Sometimes people lose precious time just emulating things they've seen before. I think when I am at a Cannes Festival or when I look at communication arts books, they are both basically graveyards. You can't write Beethoven by going to a museum or visiting his tomb. You have to go back and see why he became what he became. I'd rather learn where people started than where they ended, because at the start is where you learn. What they did at the end does not have much to do with what you are going to be in your life. When I see a great ad I can learn how to execute it, but I can not learn why the developer did it. That's the secret of creation. Why did you get there, not what did you do? Museums are full of what someone did. If creation was as simple as studying what has been done, there would be Goyas and Dalis all over. We don't have them because we don't know how they started and why they became Dalis and Goyas and Picassos. They became those people because they had a combination of the right attitude and the right time in their minds and the talent connected to that. Don't be in a hurry when you are young. Don't pigeonhole yourself too soon. And don't worry about or get absorbed by any early successes. You don't want to be 24 and done.

Interview with Lee Garfinkel
CHAIRMAN AND CHIEF CREATIVE OFFICER DDB NEW YORK

Q: Thank you very much for letting us come in to talk to you. We're very excited about this opportunity to talk about advertising and print advertising. Maybe we could start with what you think is a good working definition of advertising?

A: It's very important that advertising grab people's attention. But just as important, it's not just about grabbing their attention and entertaining them; advertising is about selling and once you grab their attention, then you have to sell them your product or an idea. My problem with so much advertising today is that people are losing that selling part, which is why there's so much advertising where people say, "I kind of remember the joke or the story, but I don't remember the product or the name of the product."

Q: Why do people look at advertising?

A: One, because they have to; you can't escape it. Two, when it's really good, people will search it out. In the old days, people watching television would just use the remote and change the channel. Today if it's TIVOed you just fast forward through the commercials, but when it's a good commercial people will actually stop and rewind and watch it. If that weren't true there wouldn't be so much excitement around Super Bowl advertising. So to answer your question, one is that you can't escape it. Two is that it's satisfying. If it's entertaining and it has a message that's

compelling to me, then I'll actually take the time to read it. Even the person who might say "I don't like advertising," when they're shopping for a car, they'll read more car ads. And that will go beyond media advertising. Now, thanks to the Web, they'll spend time on the Web reading more. So when you have a compelling message or you're talking about a product that the people are interested in, people will search out the information. Advertising is one of those sources of information.

Q: How do you think advertising works on people? What does it do to them?

A: Unfortunately, more often than not, it will bore them and that's probably 90% of all advertising. The other 10% you could divide into two categories. If it works well, you're interested in buying the product or the service, which is the main job of advertising. The other thing it can do is it can justify your purchase. After you buy a car, people still read the car advertising. You just want to be sure. So, it's a psychological game and reinforcement of, "Okay, you got me interested in it, now reinforce that I made the right decision." But, obviously, getting them interested to buy in the first place is the most important thing.

Q: Why do companies use print advertising?

A: There are a lot of opinions about the effectiveness of print advertising, especially with the Web right now. It's my feeling that as long as people continue to read newspapers, magazines, and print advertising, it can be one of the most powerful media that we have. I used to say, if you have a long story to tell, it's a great place to grab people's attention. You can go more in-depth than with a television commercial, for example. Now, the Web is becoming the best place to get a truly in-depth conversation with the consumer. What print can do is tease me to get more information and it is great for anyone who needs a deeper story. I also think it's that, in the last 10 or 15 years, print has become a lot more design-focused, and that's a bad thing. Just because you have interesting art or photography doesn't mean that you have a good ad. No matter what the medium, advertising is driven by "the big idea." If anything, this is even more important today because people multitask when they consume media. Maybe it's harder to read a magazine or newspaper and multitask, but we are learning how to even do that. When I take the train in the morning and I know

I have an ad in the newspaper, I have a focus group with 50 people. You can see how quickly they turn the page when they get to your ad. It can be devastating. You've just spent, say, $40,000 to get a full-page ad in *The New York Times* and in less than a second someone has turned the page—that's failure. On the other hand, if you can get them to stop and actually read what you have there, that's success. And my experience has been that you are not going to get that purely with fancy art direction or interesting design. You've got to have a great concept. That's what the best print ads have.

Q: Are certain appeals better made in print than in TV or online? Does print present any unique opportunities when you are trying to get across certain types of messaging?

A: You have the potential to get deeper into a subject in print. I urge my clients to get across only one notion in television. You can throw a lot of things at the consumer, but they can't take more than one main point in a 30-second television commercial. In print, you should have one main point of view, but you have an opportunity, once you grab them with your headline, to give them additional information. That's one of the nicer things you can do with print advertising. So I don't know if it's a specific appeal as much as it is the opportunity print gives you to go deeper into the subject.

Q: When you think about a campaign that runs in print, television, and online, let's say, how do you think about those media all working together? Should the messaging be the same? Should the format and the look be the same? When you think about how a campaign works across media, what works best?

A: The best thing is to have one idea that's strong enough to work in all the media. I used to judge advertising by asking myself, "Will it work in television, radio, and print?" Now, it's "Will it work in television, radio, print, Internet, telephone?"—all the new media. I'm big on what I call inventing new media. We are beyond simple considerations about traditional versus nontraditional media. I try to push everybody—our creative people, our planners, our account people—to come up with new media ideas as well—to surprise people with the media in addition to the message.

In terms of how I look at it to make sure it's right with different media, I look at the idea, and I try to

quickly get to where I can say, "Okay, I can see that in print, I can see that online, I can see that on TV." That tells me whether we are on to something. If I say, "This is pretty good on TV, but I don't have a clue about how you're going to do that in print," it probably means that the idea isn't as good as it should be; it's probably more executional. It doesn't mean we don't pursue that sometimes, but it's not the ultimate of what we like to do.

So the first thing always is, "Do we have a big idea?" Then everybody would love to be able to say that you could almost do the identical thing in television and radio. That happens sometimes. You come up with an idea that works the same in TV, print, radio, and online. More often, you then have to ask, "How could we execute this properly in the different media so that people say 'Yes, I get it.'" It's the same campaign; it may not be identical, but you get that it's of the same campaign. There was a great spot done in the '80s by Federal Express, the fast-talker commercial. If you take the notion of "We'll get there and we'll deliver this package, no matter what," and execute it in print, it may not feel exactly the same, but the strategy and the big idea are the same.

Q: Companies do a lot of segmentation; some do very narrow segmentation. How does that influence your big idea and the kind of advertising you create?

A: Well, it really depends on the client. For example, one of our clients is the New York Lottery. There's a lot of different cultures in New York and when we do a lottery spot, we try to come up with a spot that is not only going to work for New York City residents, but also for everybody in New York State. There's a very big Hispanic market in New York, so almost every TV and radio spot and print ad that we do has a Spanish version of it. We have to make sure that everything we do is not going to just resonate with English-speaking people, but resonate with Hispanics and also we're thinking more and more about the Asian community now because you don't want to have different messaging. You want the same message. For example, we just did a Lottery spot based on a character that they created 10 years ago whose name is Ralph. He's the guy who announces what the New York Lottery is, "The New York Lottery is now 8 million dollars." The new spot presented Ralph as the ultimate announcer. He is in a diner where the famous announcers are, like, Ed McMahon from Johnny Carson, the announcer from *Jeopardy,* the guy that does all the voices for the movies, and they do all of their lines. Then Ralph comes out with what the latest Lotto jackpot is. For the Spanish market, we took those announcers out because they weren't famous in the Latin community and we brought in three Spanish-speaking actors. But, because they weren't famous announcer lines, the script change was just famous lines. So they talk about this in a famous pickup line in the Hispanic community. And then, of course, none of those lines compares to the line, "The Lotto jackpot is . . ." That Hispanic version needed to be changed a little, but it's still within that same feeling and we were able to shoot it all in one day and just change the three actors. It's probably the furthest we've gone from a concept. Usually we redo a commercial almost verbatim, but in Spanish.

Market segmentation is something we absolutely think about for many of our clients. The key is to not water down the concept to the lowest common denominator. There has been a tendency in global advertising, for example, when you need something that's going to work in France and England and New York and the Middle East, to ask what they have in common. Getting down to the lowest common denominator can end up being a very boring advertisement. That doesn't have to be the result, and it's amazing how many people like a spot that you didn't necessarily even plan to be global but it really resonates for several markets. Years ago, I did a Pepsi commercial with Cindy Crawford. It was the first Cindy Crawford commercial where she gets out of a car and these two little kids see her drinking Pepsi. Everybody who sees it, it doesn't matter what country or where you're from, everybody just loves the commercial because it was sexy and charming and it was nice, and it made you feel good about Pepsi. If you're talking to a wide group of people the idea doesn't have to be watered down.

Q: Is working with online more like working with TV or more like print or is it its own thing?

A: It's a combination of all and it's its own thing. I've seen print ads where I say let's animate that online. I've seen TV commercials where I've said we're stuck with 30 seconds on TV, but we don't have a time limit online so let's make that into a 45-second piece online. The opportunity of online is one of the things that gets me really excited about being in advertising now. Many of the ideas we had years ago, we didn't know what to do with. We asked, "Where are you going to

put that?" You needed 90 seconds or that kind of form didn't exist then. Today, everything can go online. It goes back to the old story—what's the big attention-getting idea that's going to give them a message and make them search it out? With the millions of websites people go to these days, why would someone go to *your* website? When they're already in the market for a certain product and looking for as much information as possible they will search you out. But, if you're already not predisposed to buy that product or that brand, how do I get you to my site? That's really difficult, but what an opportunity. The opportunities of YouTube, where people will watch my commercials and people pass them around and make videos out of them. We did a Diet Pepsi spot last year where we took footage of football players and we dubbed them all in. Instead of talking about what the play was, we had them all talking about Diet Pepsi. We didn't put it on YouTube but somebody saw it and put it on YouTube, and just watch people rate it and comment on it. People were doing their own versions with football clips and dubbing them in. It was great. So in a way, online is its own thing, but it also is a combination of so much that you've done in the past.

Q: Some people talk about advertising being rational or emotional. Is that a distinction that makes any sense to you?

A: It depends on the product. There are different ways to sell different products. The best advertising will have a combination of the two, rational and emotional. Take cars again. Most people think they're making a rational decision when they buy a car. But emotion plays into it a lot. Take a Toyota and a Lexus; some of them are seen as functionally very much the same vehicles when you do blind side-by-side quality ratings. But the Lexus might be $5000 to $10,000 more. Rationally, they're both good cars, so I should buy the Toyota. But if my heart wants a Lexus, for whatever reasons, I'm going to buy that Lexus. So most of the time, depending on the product, the best advertising uses a combination of rational and emotional appeals, because both influence how people make buying decisions.

Q: Please describe how your agency goes about creating a print ad. How does that process work?

A: It starts with figuring out what's the client's business objective and what's its advertising objective, which are sometimes the same, but sometimes they are different. You get it to the point of answering, "What do you want this ad to do?" That's step one. Step two is answering the question of "What's the most compelling argument that you can make?" This leads to the strategy. That is *the* most important thing you can do. There must be a compelling argument of why someone should buy your product. You can almost imagine that you're a door-to-door salesman and you've knocked on somebody's door and you're going to read them the brief and by reading the brief you're going to convince them to buy your product. Now, if you could actually come up with something that's compelling in that brief, then you're 50% of the way there. Then step three is to take that brief and to make it the most attention getting. Our ad is going to be in with thousands of other ads, so it must grab their attention. Go for an ad that astonishes people, but doesn't shock them. Shocking is doing something that is only attention getting. Astonishing them is giving them a point of view or a piece of information or a way to use the product that they never thought of before. The last thing is making sure that consumers know what you want them to do after they have seen the ad. With too much advertising these days, people think, "Oh that was funny, but I'm not sure what it has to do with me, or what do they want me to do?" An example I give the creative people is from years ago, I'm not going to say who it was, but someone from a big publication was sponsoring a gun control campaign and he wanted my opinion. He didn't ask me to do work on it, just wanted my opinion. And he showed me these television commercials all about these little kids who got killed by handguns. And he said, "What do you think?" I said, "It was really emotional and it's touching, but I'm not sure if they are commercials." And he said, "Why?" And I said, "Because I feel really sad and depressed, but I don't know what you want me to do. Do you want me to make sure that my neighbors don't have handguns? Do you want me to make sure that my kids don't play with handguns? Do you want me to call my congressman? Do you want me to make sure I don't have guns in my closet? I don't know what you want me to do. If all you want me to do is feel sad, you've achieved that, but what do you want me to do?" And I think that's true for a lot of advertising these days. So, grab their attention, give them something that is insightful, that they relate to themselves, and tell them what are they supposed to do next.

Q: You talked about insight. Where does the insight come from?

A: Occasionally it just comes in a second, but that hardly ever happens. Most of the time it comes with the planners, the creative people, and the account people sitting down with all the research, pulling in the client, and making sure that you talked about everything that you can think of, brainstorm in all directions. Then the planner goes back and articulates what they think is the insight, even if, as sometimes happens, it was not said in the meeting. When it's working well, the planner will then come back and present that brief or insight strategy to the creative people and then they will fight it out again to make sure that they truly believe that it *is* insightful and compelling *and* that they can execute it easily. I know I'm in trouble if a planner reads a brief to me, and I don't see any pictures in my head. It might sound really smart and have a lot of "advertisingese" in it and will make a good meeting, and the client might like it, but if it's not sparking creative, then it's not a good brief. Some of the best briefs I've been involved in came about by accident. People will say things to one another and not realize what they're saying and inspire another idea. A planner came back from a research session and said, "I don't have any ideas." This was for motor oil. The client wanted us to say that this particular motor oil was used by the experts, which is one of the oldest strategies there is—approved by experts, used by experts. So the planner came back from interviewing a lot of guys who change their own motor oil, and he said, "I don't have any ideas, but I'll tell you one thing, those guys that change their own motor oil, they are pretty macho guys." The observations led to the insight. It led to us thinking that we're not only going to say that these guys are experts, but that there's something a little more macho about the guy who uses this motor oil. That was the twist. He didn't know that he had it, but that insight drove the advertising for several years. That ad was actually for Valvoline Motor Oil. And the insight became, "You can always tell the guys who use Valvoline."

Q: When you look at a print ad, how do you evaluate it; how do you judge whether it's a strong ad or not?

A: I start with the same things as if I were creating it. First, is it attention getting? Would I stop to read it? Second, do I find it compelling? Then, am I jealous? And then I go back to the brief and make sure it addresses all these other things that we said were important like, "Does it meet the business objective? The advertising objective?" If it does all that, it's a go and I'll fight for it.

Q: When you look at a print ad, do you kind of look at the whole and stop there or do you examine into the pieces or parts of it? If it works as a whole, is that enough?

A: I will first look at it as a whole and that's what I ask the clients to do, too. Judge it as a consumer does. We can always fix the little things. Then I'll step back, start to pick at the details, make sure that things like the pitch, type size, how the copy is written, are all right. The more I like it, the more I'll pick at it because I'll really want it to be excellent. When I started, I worked for someone who was a great operator. He would actually put the ad down on the floor and walk 20 feet back. He was a perfectionist and he just wanted to be sure that, any which way you looked at the ad, it was going to be perfect. It was a great lesson. An ad can take up two weeks of your time. Some can take a year. The more time you invest in it, the more important it becomes. You don't want to see that guy on the train zipping through your ad quickly.

Q: Do you typically create more than one ad for a brief at a time, or do you try to get to that one best ad?

A: There may have been a time many, many years ago, when we would show just one ad to the client, but that doesn't happen today. I would say that today the average is to show three ads, but it can be as many as 10 ads. There's good and bad in that. Instead of trying to come up with one really good ad for a meeting, you've got to come up with 3 or 6 or 10 really good ads for a meeting. Any ad you show needs to be viable because the client could buy any one of what you show. You don't want the client to run a bad ad and you don't want to get into a discussion of why you may have shown a bad ad. This is most likely to occur when the client has asked you to take something into consideration that you don't really believe in. You sometimes have to fight the feeling that it is okay to include something that is not very good because it is what the client asked for. Sometimes the ad is really, really excellent, you know. Most of the time, it's a B plus or an A minus, although it can be hard to differentiate between ads at that level.

Q: What makes a great creative person?

A: If we are talking about a writer, it's not just about being imaginative; you've got to be really smart. I know a lot of really imaginative people who just can't do good advertising. It's that marriage of creativity and common sense and wisdom and insight and being able to understand what will draw people's attention. People come in and present things to me and say, "Hey, don't you think this is really funny?" and I say, "Yeah, but it's not advertising." People come in with a headline that will be exactly what the strategy was and say, "Well, it's exactly on brief," and I say, "Yeah, but it's not compelling, it's not interesting so the consumer is not going to read it." The best creative people are the ones who can understand the brief, who can execute the brief, and who can come up with interesting ways to present it. They have to be both artists and businesspeople. They can't just be creative people.

I sometimes argue that I don't need to test my work because I have a really good gut instinct. Most people answer, "You have a really good track record, but now it's untested. I can't count on you 100%." I am not saying we should get rid of testing, because we learn a lot from testing, but when clients use it as a crutch instead of a guidepost, then we can get into trouble. An ad that has been approved in the gut of a chairman of a company who had the vision to create the company has a better chance of being successful than the one that went through the whole testing process, which can bring things back down to the lowest common denominator.

Q: What advice do you have for a young person thinking that he or she would like to be creative? Is it a good profession for someone today? How would you advise them to begin their education and gain experience?

A: I would definitely advise it as a profession and I would advise them to begin by becoming a jack of all trades. I was a cartoonist, I was a writer, I played guitar, I did stand-up comedy, I wrote for comics, I wrote plays, I wrote songs. I majored in communications, but I didn't study advertising at all. It wasn't until I graduated that I began to put together a portfolio. I took out books from the library and I taught myself. I took out Ogilvy's book and how-to books and I was lucky enough to meet people. I sent out résumés and kept calling. I met some good career directors who gave me advice on how to put a portfolio together, and eventually I got a job. It was great. I didn't know I could use music, comedy, writing, and art. I did not know there was a job for me, but it turned out it was perfect. As a creative director I get to use everything. So my advice to kids today is that if you're talented and you want to use a lot of different talents, and especially with the Internet right now there are so many opportunities for you to express yourself, then I would say that advertising is for you. If it's purely about art and imagination, then it may not be for you. But if you have common sense and a little real-world business savvy and are creative, then it's definitely the business for you. I've enjoyed all of it.

Q: How did you get into advertising?

A: My story is unusual because I didn't know anything and I taught myself. From the time I started my portfolio to my first job took 10 months. During that time I did nothing but work on my portfolio. My social life was dead. I was living at home. My mother and father were very supportive. I worked harder on that portfolio than I ever did in school. When I got into advertising, I continued that. I said, "If I'm in this now, I want to be good at it so I'm just going to keep going." Some people who worked for me at DDB have followed me around from agency to agency. I have a lot of people who worked for me, some for over 25 years. They will always ask every time they join me at a new place, "Can I get a raise because I know how hard you're going to work me?" I say, "No, you're not going to get a raise, but if you want to enjoy what you are doing come along." It takes a lot of work to deal with advertising.

I don't think today you do it by yourself as much. Back then, I could draw my own layouts. I was a cartoonist, but I drew my own layouts. I found an art director who did a couple of nicer ones for me. But today everybody's portfolio is from what they learned in school and on the computers. They look as good as ads. In my day I started with, "Is the idea good?" When you went for a job, they kind of overlooked that it was not great art direction because you were a beginner. But today with everybody coming out of school, the ideas have to be good and it has to look great. Sometimes the look overshadows the ideas, judging by the portfolios I've seen over the last couple of years. Competition is so strong. I may look at 250 books for the one or two that I ask to come into the agency for an interview. Because of this fierceness, the only way to compete today may be to go to school

and take courses at the different advertising schools and put the best portfolio together. Of course, having a connection in advertising can help, too.

Q: So, do you have to have a portfolio to get in the door at this point? How good does it need to be and what else do you look for?

A: A portfolio may be more important on the art director's side, but everybody knows that the writers and the art directors work together. So today's writers' books look as good as the art directors' books. The portfolio has to be really presentable because more often than not the book is going to come up to the Creative Director or the Creative Service Manager and they will go over it very quickly without the person being there, so you won't be able to editorialize or comment on your work. The book basically has to speak for itself. Similarly, let's say you are going to put 12 ads in the book (back when I started it was to be just ads; now everybody's putting everything in their book), you better have 12 really good ads in the book because if you have 12 ads and 10 are great and 2 are bad, you will get judged by your 2 weakest ads. After the book, in the interview what I look for is enthusiasm and eagerness. All things being equal, I'm looking for the person who's really willing to work hard because, let's say he did come up with a good ad and then a client kills it, I still need him to put out the same exact energy the next day when we have to go back for the second meeting. We call ourselves "Advertising Animals."

Q: You worked at how many different agencies?

A: I've worked at six agencies, but most of my previous career has been spent at three—Levine, Huntley for 11 years, Lowe for nine years, and BBDO for three years. All the agencies have been different. There have been similarities, but they've all been different. I have enjoyed them all.

Interview with Tim Mellors
PRESIDENT AND CHIEF CREATIVE OFFICER
GREY WORLDWIDE

Q: How would you define advertising? What does advertising mean today?

A: Advertising has become a slightly tarnished word. Advertising started out as a paid display of your product or service to which people reacted. And because the medium in which you did it was initially either print and then radio or television, it was very easy to see what advertising was. It's much more difficult to see or even describe what advertising is now. It's still some kind of paid communication; to promote a service or goods. But now it has moved into a new whole area. Where does PR start? What kind of publicity does advertising cover? Advertising has been superseded by a synonym, which is *marketing.*

Q: What does advertising do?

A: Think about it this way. If you had a society, like Russia was at one time, that forbade any kind of paid for advertising other than propaganda, you could ask, "What is lost in that?" What is lost is the ability to create brands or identities or products or services. If there were no branded airlines, which one would you go for? Or if beers all had the same name—they were just beer—how would you decide? There's something about projecting yourself into it. A brand is a character that enriches people's lives. Advertising defines that brand.

Q: How do you know whether an ad will be effective?

A: The short answer is I don't. I've worked on ads I just intuitively know would work. I've worked on ads that researched unbelievably well and surprised me because I didn't think they were that strong. And I've created campaigns I thought would work brilliantly and absolutely bombed in the research. So, unfortunately for the advertiser, there is a lot of uncertainty in this business. And I am not sure it will ever be any different.

Q: Do you have an example of advertising that has succeeded beyond your expectations?

A: Over as long a career as mine, we've sold lots of product. Perhaps the most interesting and odd example occurred when I was creative director for Saatchi & Saatchi. The account was British Airways, our largest. British Airways then went to 60 countries, so you have to have a relatively simple idea to execute on, such as the world's favorite airline. Within a commercial I did, I wanted to use David Bowie's track about a spaceman—Major Tom. I got in touch with him and we got it going, but at the last moment another writer who had a credit pulled his permission and we had to change the music. We wanted to save the film which had been expensive to shoot, so I tried on about 20 other tracks. Since my wife is an opera fan, one of them was a little-known piece called "The Flower Duet" from *Lakme.* It seemed to work pretty well. I brought the ad to John King, who ran British Airways, and he said "Yes, I like that and we'll use that music now as our music henceforth." And now, nearly 20 years later, if you go on a British Airways aircraft that's the music they play at the beginning. So what does that mean? It means firstly that King had a better idea of his own airline than I did. It means that if you get something subtle right, it can create an image that goes beyond its constituent parts. It means that advertising has a lot of chance in it. I'd like to tell you that I was the clever person who thought that this must be the right thing for this airline, but it wasn't like that. I see this as a motif for how many ideas work. It very much is a combined effort. His marketing director was equally keen. They'd done enough research to know the nature of what they needed to push for British Airways. That track wouldn't have worked for Virgin or the old TWA or Pan Am.

Q: Why do people do print advertising today?

A: Advertising started in print and the first users were department stores. If you look at the very first ads by Claude Hopkins and people like him, they were, some would say, *simplistic,* but I'd prefer to say *simple,* advertisements that put over a point of view firstly about the product on offer, but sometimes more about the company itself. That's unchanged over the years. Even today I'm amazed at the number of full-page ads there are for Neiman-Marcus or Barney's. The same companies that basically started the advertising are still doing glamorous pictures of watches. Why? Not to sell the particular watch—there isn't enough trade for a $6,000 watch—it's to sell the image of the store. It's to sell the fact that there's something glamorous and interesting there. And that hasn't changed in 70 years. That's the basis of print advertising.

Q: Do some messages work better in a print environment than they do in other media environments?

A: What comes to my mind first is Gap advertising, which revitalized the print medium by showing the garment in an attractive way. A photographer who works in the medium of fashion knows how to take a picture that whets the appetite of the buyer in a way that is quite unique. It has immediacy. If you're selling a suit for a dollar off this week it's an instant way to get the message across. Although people read newspapers less and tend to look online for news, those who look at newspapers heed the immediacy of these offers. However, this has not been a medium that has been very good at selling tangible items like gas.

Q: And what about magazines?

A: Magazines are the softer sister of newspapers. Magazines purport to be about news, but in fact they go into the depth of news stories or offer an opinion. Advertising within a magazine needs to have this same, more oblique, approach. The knock-me-down-drag-out ads don't work as well in magazines because you're seeing the advertisement in a different frame of mind. You tend to dip in and out. People buy magazines to have a more conscious feeling of enjoyment out of reading it than they do a newspaper.

Q: Magazines used to be a strong number two to television for advertisers. Will magazines continue to be a viable medium?

A: I would hate it if there were no magazines. I'm at an age where I don't live by them and I use the Net a lot, but there is nothing like sitting by the fire reading a magazine. Some magazines have a unique intelligence to them. Other magazines are more nonsensical. That's a very personal view. A more cold-hearted view is that their relevance will be reduced as television becomes less intelligent, more predictable, more of a common denominator. One of the things that is very noticeable about YouTube and My Space is their innate intelligence and wicked sense of fun that a younger audience tends to get. Ultimately the Net will face the same problems as TV and magazines because it will also become a means of mass communication and a means of mass selling. At the moment the older types of media—television and magazines and newspapers—are leaving the back door open to the newer medium for that kind of communication.

Q: What makes a magazine ad different from other media advertising or is there a difference?

A: I use the analogy of relationships. Television is like your family. It's part of you. You hardly notice it most of the time but it's there. New media, particularly the Net, is like your girlfriend or boyfriend.

It's very engaging. You can see no wrong in it. You lean forward. You're locked on. Magazines are like people that are familiar and yet sometimes surprising. They're like people you admire and you have an on-off relationship with them. They're not totally with you like your family is. You're not engaged with them in the same way as you are in the choice of being on the Net. So you can take them or leave them. That's quite a good proposition, in a way. People like things they can take or leave. They like the in-and-out nature of magazines. And in-and-out seems to be within the DNA of magazines.

Q: Which of the media are more personal?

A: Many say the Web because of its nature. You make a conscious effort. You physically log on and you choose where to go. You are engaged by a new world. If you dig deeper into it, though, it is my belief that it isn't as engaging and isn't as personal. It is actually quite depersonalizing. Think of how e-mail has stopped physical communication. It is very difficult to read an e-mail. "Read" as in read the persona, read the facial expression, read the intent behind an e-mail. That to me is a marker for the Web, in total. Somebody doesn't come up to you in a magazine and start shaking you by the hand. In magazines, the physical act of your turning the page over and then going back again, engages you in a more personal way.

Q: Why is copy being reduced in print ads?

A: If you look at the print advertisements that have been shown at the Cannes Festival in the last four or five years, they are mostly one-liners, which shows how creative people think of the medium. These are ads basically done by designers that have a headline and that have a very interesting picture. If any copy, it's very short, often one line. Last year, I counted the ads that had more than one line. There were three out of something like three hundred. This shows that long copy is dead and gives you an indication of how people approach the print medium. When I started, I worked on the Volkswagen account, which was the agency's cream account. You had to write three paragraphs, three columns of copy the exact length to fit the layout that had been done with the certain style of width. It was a bit like learning Latin at school. It was prescribed and it worked in a particular way. There was a huge sense of satisfaction to be able to solve the crossword puzzle and to write within the vernacular of a particular advertising style. There is no equivalent of that now, at least verbally or word-wise. There is a visual style that is the vernacular and that is often quite surreal. The use of surrealism in advertising and visual surrealism has become commonplace and there is a whole kind of thinking behind it that is completely unconscious by the people who do it.

I don't know the reason for this, but it may have to do with us having become the most visually literate group of people that's ever been on Earth. We are bombarded with images. This rich visual experience means you have to compete very hard to get a stunning image. But when you get it, it's effortless in engaging. The problem with a piece of copy is that you have to read it. And the longer it is, the longer you have to read. This also in a time in which short-termism seems to win. If you can do something in two seconds, why take one minute or two minutes to read it? Another reason is more pragmatic. English is only just the first language and shortly won't be. Spanish is just behind and soon will overtake it. Assume there are just two languages even though there are many more. What happens is that you need to write in a way that works in both languages. Now, quite often you are making a commercial that will run in 20 countries. You've got to get it pretty simple so it's easily translated, and one of the things you are going to give up is nuanced information or explanation.

Q: How do you create an ad? What is the mechanical process?

A: One of the most profound changes in this business, in fact in journalism, is the arrival of the Mac or PC. I was brought up with metal type, which had to be sent out. I was brought up with physical proofs, and if you did titles, they too were sent away to a title house. Now everything can be done almost instantaneously and by yourself. I can shoot and edit my own stuff. I can get a camera that fits in my hand and it can be HD quality. I can edit it in my computer. I can take some music down from the ether and create a track. I can get a picture from a website that specializes in pictures, put it in a layout, edit it with my protocol, find out what the size of the magazine is, find out the length that's been bought for the commercial. I can literally run the whole thing from that computer sitting on that desk. This has shortened the lead time, the chain of operation, enormously.

Q: Do art directors and copywriters work in teams anymore?

A: The schools still train art designers and copywriters, but there is more flexibility between the two skill sets. I started working on magazines and was an art director initially. Then, I wrote for newspapers. So I was both an art director and a writer. That was unusual then, now it's almost the norm. In fact, more designers come into the business as art directors or art people. Training in pure copy is almost a waste of time now, I'm afraid. Many people argue this is a bad thing because it's a discipline taught in communication. One of the unique things about advertising is the idea of the creative team. At first, copywriters sat in one part of the building and the visualizers, as we called them, sat in a studio and you just pushed the copy under the door, a bit like a newspaper and they illustrated it. Then we got the two together and worked them in teams. A team is far greater than its constituent parts. One of the things that's overlooked is that you bring your life into the room and sit with another person whom you often know better than your own wife or husband or best friend. In the creative process you're bringing your knowledge of the world into the room and it aligns with another person's, and what comes out is some combination of both. So we still tend to work in teams or pairs, but they're not as demarcated as they used to be.

Q: How important is it for you to know the target audience? Do you create differently depending on who those audiences are? How do you do that?

A: Almost everything I know about selling can be learned from a person at a store in a market. One thing that you will notice about someone selling fruit, vegetables, or clothes or second-hand goods is that they know their market. They're able to assess intuitively what will work against a particular group or person. A really good creative person intuitively knows that as well. You can get it really wrong if you talk the same to a college kid as you do to a gray-haired 70 year old pensioner. That's the intuitive part. Then there's the more informed part. Any creative problem is solvable. You listen to a planner or research person who will make you more intimate with the nuances beneath the broader typology. If it's a college person, what is she studying? What are her interests? A college person who's studying botany and is a fisherman and a baseball fan is not the same as a college person who's on a basketball scholarship who likes Japanese food and rap and drives a Jeep. The more I know about the people, the more accurate I can be. To me, advertising is a process of mirroring. I see the person I'm selling to, and I try to couch it and promote it in the language and the posture that I know will work best for that person. At its best, it's a brilliant skill, but it's an inexact science.

Q: When you are presented with an ad to approve, how do you know if it will work?

A: The only way I know is by experience, and I'm probably right only between 50% and 70% of the time. I also try to put myself into the audience's position. If I were a consumer, how would I feel about what I am seeing?

Q: Do you evaluate an ad as a whole or do you give feedback about most of its parts?

A: I look at the whole. I see the field. I see everything that's in it. Then when I accept that I examine the details. Sometimes, by changing the details in the foreground, it changes the gestalt. It changes the picture. But unless you get the impact of the whole right you never get to the details. I'm very quick at judging things. If something's wrong I feel it right away. In general, that which strikes you as good the first time tends to be quite good and tends to work better than that which you argue into a box and say "This is what the client said; this is what the research said."

Q: What do you look for in creative candidates? What kind of skills should they have? What kind of experience do you think they should have?

A: People I hire have changed massively over the years. When I was in England, I used to hire bright college people who've done an arts degree to write and art college people who've done a degree in art to be art directors. Now I am miles outside of that. I look for people with absolutely various backgrounds. Recently, I started an agency within an agency. None of the people I have hired so far has an advertising background. They come from the Comedy Channel, flash animators, two from a fashion school, a guy who's in the music business, a woman who's straight from Yale and is just bright. I follow my instinct and I look for whatever creativity they show. It's the ability to draw from the whole experience. One of the reasons

for that, I believe, is this whole Internet generation is equally more inclusive and unorthodox. I am trying to mirror that with the kind of people whom I hire.

Q: Do they have a portfolio?

A: Some do, some don't. I ask them a number of questions. I explain what we do here. I show some work. I ask what they know about advertising and advertisements. I judge on the basis of that. That's not to say I haven't hired a lot of people with advertising backgrounds. It just happens that this group I've brought in for their skill in the interactive area, I'd be hard pressed to come up with any commonality, even musically or films that they like. When you work with them you get to know what they're like, you get to know their backgrounds. And I team them up off and on with each other. Sometimes four work together, but usually it's two and it's not the same two all the time. Sometimes they clash and sometimes they don't, but you work with a partner on each project.

Q: For someone thinking about getting into advertising, what do you advise them to do or to study?

A: I would advise them to not just think "I'd like to get into advertising." Instead think of all the media, all the ways you can communicate with people. There is a richer variety of that than there's ever been. And, if possible, don't select one of those until you have to. Absolutely load yourself up on images and information, input, and taking in as much as you can. When you do, the opportunities arise. It's very nonlinear and different from the mainstream American educational system, which is based on a kind of linear decision-making process where you make choices that narrow down your options. Think instead of the Rudolph Steiner model of education, which is a holistic approach where you take in as much information as you possibly can and try to connect things. Why is a leaf shaped like a hand? Why are the digits the same as the bones? When a leaf blows, why does it blow in a particular way? What's it got to do with a leaf? How does wind work? What happens as the world climate warms? Will that make a difference to how airplanes stay up or the way leaves go or your bones work? To me, that kind of seemingly irrelevant knowledge is probably the most relevant knowledge for understanding communication. Otherwise, we will head toward a saturation point where communication is only done at its most common level. Businesses die unless they embrace the new values that people bring to them. If you shamelessly sell a new product, people become suspicious. If you try to fool them, eventually they won't buy. This is a new, choosier, more educated, more antisell group of people than there's ever been. You have to come up with ways to engage them that's never been done. Craig's List is a wonderful example of an amazing and simple piece of new advertising. It is based on having consumers bring our knowledge to the marketer, rather than have the marketer impart knowledge to the consumer.

Probably one of the things that is killing copy is its very lexicon, the way we have expressed ourselves. It was a clever and elaborate collection of words, basically, the same language people on the news use. It speaks in a particular way. It's not American or English. It's "Newsism." It gets your attention but it doesn't tell you anything more. It's our job to develop a new way to communicate and engage. Selling needn't be heavy and inevitable. That is a problem that advertisers can't ignore.

Q: What is an example of the types of projects that your new group works on?

A: Procter & Gamble makes Febreze, an antiodor product. It's a big product. We came up with an idea that said, "Well, people in college smell. They live in little dorm rooms. They don't wash their clothes very often. Surely, that's a fantastic opportunity." We were right, but you can't just run a 30-second commercial or print ad to communicate to this group. We decided to recommend something different. We'll get this group, this comedy troupe that goes around to universities and we'll send them out on the What Stinks Tour. They'll talk about political things that stink, things in art that stink. But they can also talk about their roommate and who's the dirtiest in the dorm. Get it in their language. Now, that's not very conventional, but Procter & Gamble is a very smart marketer. If they can bring in customers one or even two generations early, they have enlarged their market substantially. So the people at Procter researched it, and confirmed it to be a great idea. We turned the message into the vernacular of the audience. So we energized something somewhat mundane and dull by constructing a new use for it and speaking in a new language. I went with the team to Cincinnati to sell the idea because I believed in it and because I wanted to make sure it didn't get lost—and it didn't.

The company did a market test and now it's gone out nationally. The program we ended up with does sampling, a traditional pop thing. We send out The Upright Citizens Brigade, they did *Saturday Night Live* originally, to do the show. It doesn't have any references to Febreze other than a banner "Presented by Febreze." And then we do a sampling at the same time. It's about what stinks in life. What do you think stinks? "I think this campus stinks. This college stinks." We don't edit any of it because it's not for general audiences. It's something for them to engage in. And we put it out on the Net where they can send in or blog their ideas and send in pictures.

Q: How do you reach or handle something like that?

A: Through the Net. We couldn't do the whole campaign through the Upright Citizens Brigade. It would be too expensive. But with the Net, it builds its own word of mouth, which is the most valuable thing of all. Students come from different schools to colleges, but they're on with each other. Facebook. YouTube. Blogs. They're on the Net saying, "I saw this band today. I saw this comedy troupe. . . ." Reach is multiplied exponentially.

The Following 20 Sets of Consumer Advertisements Were Tested by Gallup & Robinson

EXAMPLE 1

Courtesy of Unilever.

A

Go from prickly to pretty in 1.6 ox. flat. we make Dove deodor-ant with 1/4 moisturizer to make those bumpy, razor-burned armpits smooth and lovely. it's something the most discrimi-nating spaghetti straps will appreciate.

Courtesy of Unilever.

B

What if shaving under your arms felt good? Dove deodorant makes irritated, just-shaved armpits feel so much better. 1/4 moisturizer calms and smoothes angry skin, leaving it soft and pretty—like it's meant to be. You'll look at your razor in a whole new way.

EXAMPLE 1

Size/color:	Both ads were 1-page, 4-color ads.
Test magazines:	Ad A—*Glamour,* Fall
	Ad B— *Cosmopolitan,* Spring
Magazine type:	*Glamour* is edited for the contemporary American woman. It informs her of the trends, recommends how she can adapt them to her needs, and motivates her to take action. More than half of *Glamour*'s editorial content focuses on fashion, beauty and health, and the coverage of personal relationships, travel, career, food, and entertainment.
	Cosmopolitan is edited for young women of today, dealing with the emotional side of their lives. Articles include such issues as relationships, careers, science, money, travel, fashion beauty, beauty, food, and decorating. Also there are celebrity profiles and fiction.
Assignment:	Which ad performed better among women and why do you think so?

STUDENT ANALYSIS

NAME_____ CLASS_____ DATE_____

EXAMPLE 2

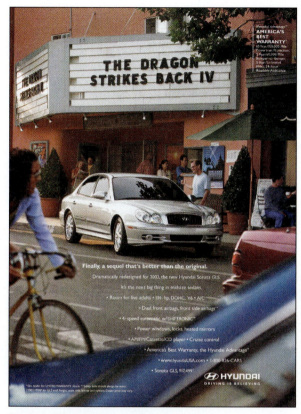

Courtesy of Hyundai Motor America.

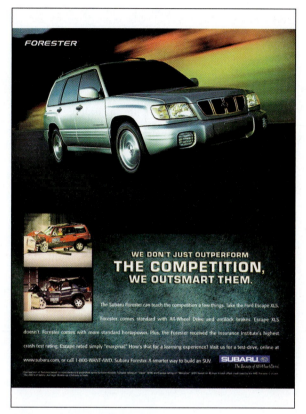

Courtesy of Subaru of America, Inc.

A

The Dragon Strikes Back IV

Finally, a sequel that's better than the original.

Dramatically redesigned for 2002, the new Hyundai Sonata GLS.

It's the next big thing in midsize sedans.

- Room for five adults
- 181-hp, DOHC, V6
- A/C
- Dual front airbags, front side airbags
- 4-speed automatic w/ SHIFTRONIC™
- Power windows, locks, heated mirrors
- AM/FM/Cassette/CD player
- Cruise control
- America's Best Warranty, the Hyundai Advantage™
- www.hyundaiUSA.com
- 1-800-826-CARS
- Sonata GLS, $17,499

B

We don't just outperform the competition, we outsmart them.

The Subaru Forester can teach the competition a few things. Take the Ford Escape XLS. Forester comes standard with All-Wheel Drive and antilock brakes. Escape XLS doesn't. Forester comes with more standard horsepower. Plus, the Forester received the Insurance Institute's highest crash test rating. Escape rated simply "marginal." How's that for a learning experience? Visit us for a test-drive, online at www .subaru.com, or call 1-800-WANT-AWD. Subaru Forester. A smarter way to build an SUV.

EXAMPLE 2

Size/color:	Both ads were 1-page, 4-color ads.
Test magazines:	Ad A—*Men's Health,* Fall
	Ad B—*Bon Appétit,* Spring
Magazine type:	*Men's Health* is the world's largest men's magazine brand, with 38 editions around the world, a monthly circulation of 1.85 million, and 12 million monthly readers. It is the best-selling men's magazine on U.S. newsstands. It covers fitness, nutrition, sexuality, lifestyle, and other aspects of men's life and health.
	Bon Appétit focuses on sophisticated home entertaining, with emphasis on food and its presentation. Also there are features on fine tableware, kitchen design, travel, and restaurants. Regular departments cover tableware and products; food-related collectables; health and nutrition; quick recipes for weekday meals; cooking techniques; wine and spirits; and recipes from restaurants, hotels, and inns around the world.
Assignment:	Which ad performed better among men and why do you think so?

STUDENT ANALYSIS

NAME_____ CLASS_____ DATE_____

EXAMPLE 3

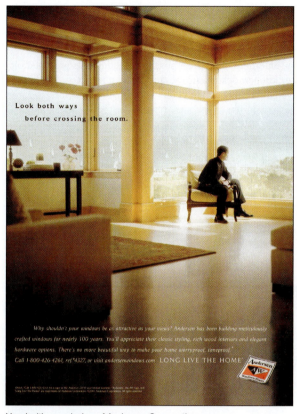

Used with permission of Andersen Corporation.

Courtesy of Pella Corporation.

A

Look both ways before crossing the room.

Why shouldn't your windows be as attractive as your views? Andersen has been building meticulously crafted windows for nearly 100 years. You'll appreciate their classic styling, rich wood interiors and elegant hardware options. There's no more beautiful way to make your home worryproof, timeproof. Call 1-800-426-4261, ref. 4327, or visit andersenwindows.com

Long live the home

B

The blinds will never get dirty. The rest of the house is another story.

Between-the-Glass Blinds from Pella. It's a small miracle for parents everywhere. After all, it's not just home improvement, it's life improvement.

1-800-54-PELLA

www.pella.com

EXAMPLE 3

Size/color: Both ads were 1-page, 4-color ads.

Test magazines: Ad A—*Bon Appétit,* Spring

                                 Ad B—*Better Homes and Gardens,* Spring

Magazine type: *Bon Appétit* focuses on sophisticated home entertaining, with emphasis on food and its presentation. Also there are features on fine tableware, kitchen design, travel, and restaurants. Regular departments cover tableware and products; food-related collectables; health and nutrition; quick recipes for weekday meals; cooking techniques; wine and spirits; and recipes from restaurants, hotels, and inns around the world.

                                 Better Homes and Gardens provides home service information for people who have a serious interest in their homes. It provides in-depth coverage of home and family subjects, including food and appliances, building and handyman, decorating, family money management, gardening, travel, health, automobiles, home and family entertainment, new product information, and shopping.

Assignment: Which ad performed better among women and why do you think so?

STUDENT ANALYSIS

NAME_____ CLASS_____ DATE_____

EXAMPLE 4

A

Regimen for success:

Push through muscle burn.

Protect against sunburn.

Outsmart razor burn.

Introducing the Xtreme 3™ for women with Vitamin E.

Triple blade closeness while avoiding razor burn.

Our triple blade disposable razors flex on a center pivot so you can shave extremely close while avoiding razor burn. The comfort strip with Vitamin E lubricates skin so blades glide easily over curves and contours.

Get close. Not burned.™

www.xtreme2.com

B

Introducing the shaver that makes shaving cream obsolete

The new Intuition™ is the only razor that lathers and shaves in one easy step.

The All-In-One™ cartridge features triple blades surrounded by a Skin Conditioning Solid.™

Just add water and the Skin Conditioning Solid creates its own light lather.

With every stroke, Intuition smooths and soothes for soft, touchable skin.

The All-In-One™ cartridge pops in and out for easy replacement.

www.schickintuition.com

1-800-SHAVERS

EXAMPLE 4

Size/color:	Both ads were 1-page, 4-color ads.
Test magazines:	Ad A—*Allure,* Summer
	Ad B—*Glamour,* Summer
Magazine type:	*Allure* is a women's beauty magazine. The magazine has different features, all based on the subject of beauty. A signature of the magazine is its annual Best of Beauty awards, a combination of readers' and editors' picks for their favorite products.
	Glamour is edited for the contemporary American woman. It informs her of the trends, recommends how she can adapt them to her needs, and motivates her to take action. More than half of *Glamour*'s editorial content focuses on fashion, beauty and health, and the coverage of personal relationships, travel, career, food, and entertainment.
Assignment:	Which ad performed better among women and why do you think so?

STUDENT ANALYSIS

NAME_____ CLASS_____ DATE_____

EXAMPLE 5

Courtesy of LG Electronics USA, Inc.

A

Suspend your disbelief.

The World's First 60" Plasma High-Definition TV

An expectation-shattering experience and only 4" deep, The Perfect Vision magazine calls the Zenith 60" Plasma "a technological achievement." Whether it's the 60", 50", 42" or 40" Plasma, one look and it's incredibly clear, Zenith is setting the standard in HDTV.

60" LCD Projection HDTV D60WLCD

Integrated HDTV C34W23

15.1" LCD HDTV ZLD15A1B

Zenith Z®

Digitize the Experience.™

Visit www.zenith.com or call 1-877-9ZENITH.

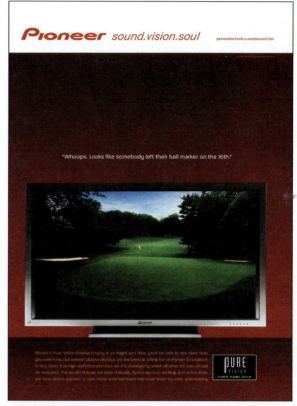

Pioneer Electronics (USA) Inc.

B

"Whoops. Looks like somebody left their ball marker on the 16th."

Pioneer's Pure Vision Plasma Display is so bright and clear, you'll be able to see more than you ever have. Our newest plasma displays are the latest in a long line of Pioneer innovations. In fact, these true high-definition monitors are the standard by which all other HD sets should be measured. The result? Dramas are more dramatic. Sports are more exciting. And action flicks are more action-packed. In fact, home entertainment has never been so, well, entertaining.

EXAMPLE 5

Size/color: Both ads were 1-page, 4-color ads.

Test magazines: Both ads were tested in *Men's Health,* Fall

Magazine type: *Men's Health* is the world's largest men's magazine brand, with 38 editions around the world, a monthly circulation of 1.85 million, and 12 million monthly readers. It is the best-selling men's magazine on U.S. newsstands. It covers fitness, nutrition, sexuality, lifestyle, and other aspects of men's life and health.

Assignment: Which ad performed better among men and why do you think so?

STUDENT ANALYSIS

NAME_____ CLASS_____ DATE_____

EXAMPLE 6

Courtesy of Audi of America, Inc.

Courtesy of Audi of America, Inc.

A

Multitronic?

Supersonic?

What if a transmission had no gears and every possible gear all at the same time? And what if it could be as fast as a manual, yet smoother and more fuel efficient than an automatic? It would be revolutionary. Which is why we created our multitronic™ CVT, the only continuously variable transmission able to handle high-torque engines. Available on Audi A4 and A6 FrontTrak® front-wheel drive models, it is yet another example of our approach toward building cars.

Never quit. Never do the expected. Never rest on your laurels. Never think great is good enough. Never follow.™

B

Unleaded Fuel?

Jet Fuel?

What happens when you get a small group of highly creative people together? They don't follow rules. They seek only to create, to surprise, to astonish. And the result? The TT Coupe and Roadster, pure sports cars so stunning in design and performance they are impossible to ignore. Available with a 180 hp or a 225 hp engine, as well as quattro® all-wheel drive, they are another example of our belief that brilliance is the result of creative vision, not corporate agreement.

Never quit. Never do the expected. Never rest on your laurels. Never think great is good enough. Never follow.™

EXAMPLE 6

Size/color:	Both ads were 1-page, 4-color ads.
Test magazines:	Ad A—*Bon Appétit,* Winter
	Ad B—*Bon Appétit,* Spring
Magazine type:	*Bon Appétit* focuses on sophisticated home entertaining, with emphasis on food and its presentation. Also there are features on fine tableware, kitchen design, travel, and restaurants. Regular departments cover tableware and products; food-related collectables; health and nutrition; quick recipes for weekday meals; cooking techniques; wine and spirits; and recipes from restaurants, hotels, and inns around the world.
Assignment:	Which ad performed better among men and why do you think so?

STUDENT ANALYSIS

NAME_____ CLASS_____ DATE_____

EXAMPLE 7

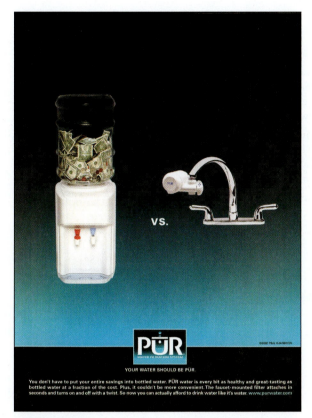

Courtesy of P&G.

A

You don't have to put your entire savings into bottled water. PŪR water is every bit as healthy and great-tasting as bottled water at a fraction of the cost. Plus, it couldn't be more convenient. The faucet-mounted filter attaches in seconds and turns on and off with a twist. So now you can actually afford to drink water like it's water.

www.purwater.com

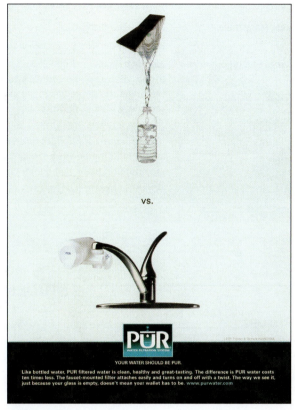

Courtesy of P&G.

B

Like bottled water, PUR filtered water is clean, healthy and great-tasting. The difference is PUR water costs ten times less. The faucet-mounted filter attaches easily and turns on and off with a twist. The way we see it, just because your glass is empty, doesn't mean your wallet has to be.

www.purwater.com

EXAMPLE 7

Size/color:	Both ads were 1-page, 4-color ads.
Test magazines:	Ad A—*People,* Fall
	Ad B—*Better Homes and Gardens,* Winter
Magazine type:	*People* focuses on compelling personalities of our time, from the known to the unknown, the famous to the infamous, the ordinary to the extraordinary. Likewise the publication serves as a guide to important developments in the arts, sciences, politics, sports, television, motion pictures, books, and records, with the spotlight on people involved in those areas.
	Better Homes and Gardens provides home service information for people who have a serious interest in their homes. It provides in-depth coverage of home and family subjects, including food and appliances, building and handyman, decorating, family money management, gardening, travel, health, automobiles, home and family entertainment, new product information, and shopping.
Assignment:	Which ad performed better among women and why do you think so?

STUDENT ANALYSIS

NAME _____ CLASS _____ DATE _____

EXAMPLE 8

A

Trash Crash #48

The banana split

Next time, use Glad® Drawstring trash bags. They're the only bags with 3-ply strength to help protect against messy breaks.

Don't get mad. Get Glad® kitchen and black trash bags.

B

Wake up and smell the coffee

Now there's Glad® large Odor Shield® trash bags. They're the only large trash bags that actually neutralize trash odors, so the only smell you'll have to face in the morning is the fresh smell of coffee.

EXAMPLE 8

Size/color:	Both ads were 1-page, 4-color ads.
Test magazines:	Ad A—*Ladies' Home Journal,* Spring
	Ad B—*Cosmopolitan,* Fall
Magazine type:	*Ladies' Home Journal* contains highly focused features and articles that reflect varied interests such as beauty and fashion, food and nutrition, health and medicine, home decorating and design, parenting, and self-help.
	Cosmopolitan is edited for young women of today, dealing with the emotional side of their lives. Articles include such issues as relationships, careers, science, money, travel, fashion beauty, beauty, food, and decorating. Also there are celebrity profiles and fiction.
Assignment:	Which ad performed better among women and why do you think so?

STUDENT ANALYSIS

NAME_____ CLASS_____ DATE_____

EXAMPLE 9

Courtesy of P&G.

A

A refreshing ocean mist now captured forever in a fragrance.

New Soft Ocean Mist™ From Downy®

It touches so much more than clothes

Courtesy of P&G.

B

Get in the mood with new Downy® Simple Pleasures™

Essences of Water Lily & Jasmine

Essences of Vanilla & Lavender

Essences of Morning Glory & Honeysuckle

Introducing a *New Collection of Fabric Softeners From Downy With Blends Of Essences* and *Natural Essential Oils*

An everyday simple pleasure for your clothes . . . and your mood.

EXAMPLE 9

Size/color:	Both ads were 1-page, 4-color ads.
Test magazines:	Ad A—*People,* Spring
	Ad B—*People,* Winter
Magazine type:	*People* focuses on compelling personalities of our time, from the known to the unknown, the famous to the infamous, the ordinary to the extraordinary. Likewise the publication serves as a guide to important developments in the arts, sciences, politics, sports, television, motion pictures, books, and records, with the spotlight on people involved in those areas.
Assignment:	Which ad performed better among women and why do you think so?

STUDENT ANALYSIS

NAME_____ CLASS_____ DATE_____

EXAMPLE 10

Courtesy of P&G.

A

Blend. Shade. Define.

Whiten.

Crest SpinBrush Pro Whitening. Its two moving heads and polishing bristles brush away stains as they clean for whiter teeth in 14 days, guaranteed. About $8. Another part of the Crest Dental Plan. Crest Healthy, Beautiful Smiles for Life.

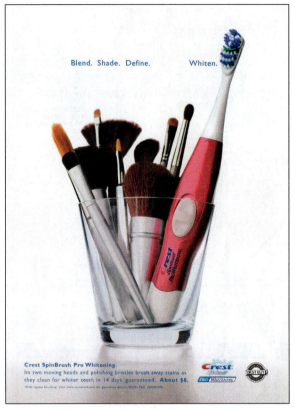

Courtesy of P&G.

B

Blend. Shade. Define.

Whiten.

Crest SpinBrush Pro Whitening.

Its two moving heads and polishing bristles brush away stains as they clean for whiter teeth in 14 days, guaranteed. About $8.

EXAMPLE 10

Size/color:	Both ads were 1-page, 4-color ads.
Test magazines:	Both ads were tested in *Cosmopolitan,* Summer
Magazine type:	*Cosmopolitan* is edited for young women of today, dealing with the emotional side of their lives. Articles include such issues as relationships, careers, science, money, travel, fashion beauty, beauty, food, and decorating. Also there are celebrity profiles and fiction.
Assignment:	Which ad performed better among women and why do you think so?

STUDENT ANALYSIS

NAME_____ CLASS_____ DATE_____

EXAMPLE 11

A

For heartburn, there's something completely different.

Only Pepcid Complete has 2 active ingredients.

Only Pepcid Complete starts to neutralize acid on contact and keeps heartburn from coming back all day or all night.

Just one and heartburn's done.

B

Heads—Fast acting.

Tails—Long lasting.

Why not choose both?

New Tums® Lasting Effects.™

It's got an instant creamy sensation. Within seconds you can feel it soothing. Then it creates a unique barrier that keeps acid away for hours. And since it's Tums, you know it has calcium. You win.

EXAMPLE 11

Size/color: Both ads were 1-page, 4-color ads.

Test magazines: Ad A—*Ladies' Home Journal,* Fall

                     Ad B—*People,* Winter

Magazine type: *Ladies' Home Journal* contains highly focused features and articles that reflect varied interests such as beauty and fashion, food and nutrition, health and medicine, home decorating and design, parenting, and self-help.

                     People focuses on compelling personalities of our time, from the known to the unknown, the famous to the infamous, the ordinary to the extraordinary. Likewise the publication serves as a guide to important developments in the arts, sciences, politics, sports, television, motion pictures, books, and records, with the spotlight on people involved in those areas.

Assignment: Which ad performed better among women and why do you think so?

STUDENT ANALYSIS

NAME_____ CLASS_____ DATE_____

EXAMPLE 12

Courtesy of Discover Financial Services.

A

Welcomed at Red Lobster® and more than 1,000 new merchants every day.

It pays to Discover.®

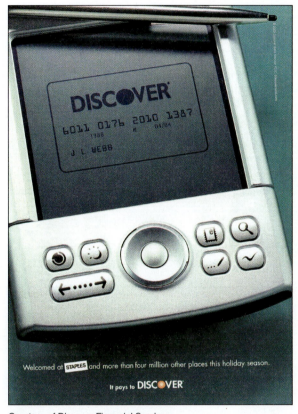

Courtesy of Discover Financial Services.

B

Welcomed at Staples® and more than four million other places this holiday season.

It pays to Discover.®

EXAMPLE 12

Size/color: Both ads were 1-page, 4-color ads.

Test magazines: Ad A—*People,* Winter

            Ad B—*Better Homes and Gardens,* Winter

Magazine type: *People* focuses on compelling personalities of our time, from the known to the unknown, the famous to the infamous, the ordinary to the extraordinary. Likewise the publication serves as a guide to important developments in the arts, sciences, politics, sports, television, motion pictures, books, and records, with the spotlight on people involved in those areas.

            Better Homes and Gardens provides home service information for people who have a serious interest in their homes. It provides in-depth coverage of home and family subjects, including food and appliances, building and handyman, decorating, family money management, gardening, travel, health, automobiles, home and family entertainment, new product information, and shopping.

Assignment: Which ad performed better among women and why do you think so?

STUDENT ANALYSIS

NAME_____ CLASS_____ DATE_____

70

EXAMPLE 13

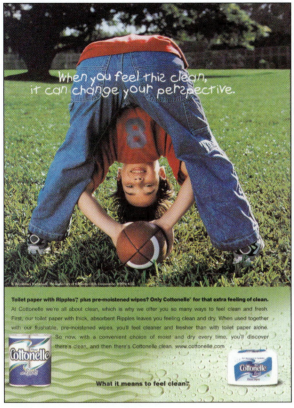

© 2008 KCWW Reprinted with Permission.

© 2008 KCWW Reprinted with Permission.

A _____

When you feel this clean, it can change your perspective.

Toilet paper with Ripples,™ plus pre-moistened wipes? Only Cottonelle® for that extra feeling of clean.

At Cottonelle we're all about clean, which is why we offer you so many ways to feel clean and fresh. First, our toilet paper with thick, absorbent Ripples leaves you feeling clean and dry. When used together with our flushable, pre-moistened wipes, you'll feel cleaner and fresher than with toilet paper alone. So now, with a convenient choice of moist and dry every time, you'll discover there's clean, and then there's Cottonelle clean. www.cottonelle.com

What it means to feel clean.™

B _____

Cottonelle.® Lab Tested for Softness.

Only Cottonelle toilet paper has thick, cushy Ripples® so it's Cottonelle® soft.

Cottonelle.® Looking out for the family.™

71

EXAMPLE 13

Size/color:	Both ads were 1-page, 4-color ads.
Test magazines:	Ad A—*Ladies' Home Journal,* Spring
	Ad B—*Better Homes and Gardens,* Winter
Magazine type:	*Ladies' Home Journal* contains highly focused features and articles that reflect varied interests such as beauty and fashion, food and nutrition, health and medicine, home decorating and design, parenting, and self-help.
	Better Homes and Gardens provides home service information for people who have a serious interest in their homes. It provides in-depth coverage of home and family subjects, including food and appliances, building and handyman, decorating, family money management, gardening, travel, health, automobiles, home and family entertainment, new product information, and shopping.
Assignment:	Which ad performed better among women and why do you think so?

STUDENT ANALYSIS

NAME_____ CLASS_____ DATE_____

EXAMPLE 14

REACH® is a registered trademark of Johnson & Johnson. Used with permission.

REACH® is a registered trademark of Johnson & Johnson. Used with permission.

A

"Miss Pomeroy, have you seen my polishing pads?"

Try these:

Our unique polishing pads are designed to remove dulling film gently, for a bright youthful smile.

Introducing the incomparable new Reach® Brightener™

Clinically proven to keep teeth their brightest

We 'borrowed' the dentist's polishing pads—or at least the idea behind them—to create the extraordinary new REACH® MAX™ Brightener toothbrush. With multi-level bristles to clean your hardest-to-reach spots—and our unique polishing pads designed to remove dulling film gently—it polishes your teeth to keep them at their brightest.

Use twice a day and keep your smile at its youthful, vibrant best.

B

To clean where bad breath hides:

Option #1: A roll-out tongue

Option #2: REACH® Fresh & Clean

Our first toothbrush with a tongue cleaner

Up to 90% of bad breath is caused by bacteria on the back of your tongue. So REACH® created Fresh & Clean, our first two-sided toothbrush and tongue cleaner that cleans all of your HARD TO REACH PLACES.™ Get fresh breath and clean teeth . . . without getting a roll-out tongue!

Nothing is beyond REACH®

EXAMPLE 14

Size/color:	Both ads were 1-page, 4-color ads.
Test magazines:	Ad A—*Cosmopolitan,* Fall
	Ad B—*People,* Fall
Magazine type:	*Cosmopolitan* is edited for young women of today, dealing with the emotional side of their lives. Articles include such issues as relationships, careers, science, money, travel, fashion beauty, beauty, food, and decorating. Also there are celebrity profiles and fiction.
	People focuses on compelling personalities of our time, from the known to the unknown, the famous to the infamous, the ordinary to the extraordinary. Likewise the publication serves as a guide to important developments in the arts, sciences, politics, sports, television, motion pictures, books, and records, with the spotlight on people involved in those areas.
Assignment:	Which ad performed better among women and why do you think so?

STUDENT ANALYSIS

NAME_____ CLASS_____ DATE_____

EXAMPLE 15

Used with permission of Volkswagen Group of America, Inc.®

A

"Hey, there's a black one."

Drivers wanted.®

Used with permission of Volkswagen Group of America, Inc.®

B

"Hey, there's a blue one."

Drivers wanted.®

EXAMPLE 15

Size/color:	Both ads were 1-page, 4-color ads.
Test magazines:	Ad A—*Men's Health,* Fall
	Ad B—*Self,* Fall
Magazine type:	*Men's Health* is the world's largest men's magazine brand, with 38 editions around the world, a monthly circulation of 1.85 million, and 12 million monthly readers. It is the best-selling men's magazine on U.S. newsstands. It covers fitness, nutrition, sexuality, lifestyle, and other aspects of men's life and health.
	Self is edited for active, professional women who are interested in improving the quality of their lives and the world they live in. The magazine provides a balanced approach to attaining individual satisfaction, with information on beauty, health, fitness, food, fashion, culture, career, politics, and the environment.
Assignment:	Which ad performed better and why do you think so?

STUDENT ANALYSIS

NAME_____ CLASS_____ DATE_____

76

EXAMPLE 16

A

With 80 calories, it's the only smoothie that's light 'n Fit.™

80 calories. 0% fat. New Dannon® Light 'n Fit Smoothie is the lightest smoothie ever, with a taste you'll love. You've never had a smoothie like this before.

Drink Light 'n Fit. Be light 'n Fit.™

Dannon.® Better every day™

www.dannon.com

B

Carb Control.™ So good . . . we bottled it!

We make every carb count.™

Now enjoy the delicious 70-calorie on-the-go smoothie with 90% less sugar than regular dairy-based smoothies. Like the cup, it's a good source of calcium and protein, and made with active yogurt cultures. It's a perfect drink wherever you are. Find out more at dannoncarbcontrol.com.

Eat Light 'n Fit. Be Light 'n Fit.™

Dannon.® Better every day®

EXAMPLE 16

Size/color:	Both ads were 1-page, 4-color ads.
Test magazines:	Ad A—*Cosmopolitan,* Summer
	Ad B— *Redbook,* Spring
Magazine type:	*Cosmopolitan* is edited for young women of today, dealing with the emotional side of their lives. Articles include such issues as relationships, careers, science, money, travel, fashion beauty, beauty, food, and decorating. Also there are celebrity profiles and fiction.
	Redbook contains features and articles on lifestyles and women's interest, and is primarily targeted toward younger married women. Features cover such topics as women dealing with hardships, aspiring for intellectual growth, and encouraging women to work together for humanitarian causes. It often profiles successful women, providing inspirational testimonies and advice on life.
Assignment:	Which ad performed better among women and why do you think so?

STUDENT ANALYSIS

NAME_____ CLASS_____ DATE_____

EXAMPLE 17

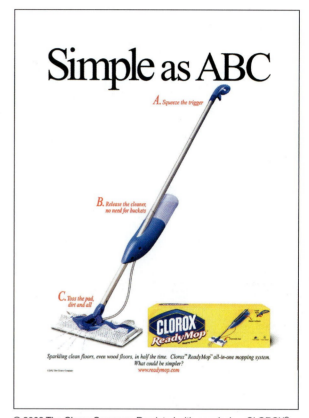

A

We wondered if Woody the Woodsman wanted a wood floor washer that worked without worry or weakness, what would woodworker Woody want?

Woodsman Woody whispered with a wink, "Well, if ol' Wily Woody wanted a wonderful wood floor, it would be wise to wield a WetJet, which works on walnut without wallowing in wood-withering water. So I don't worry while WetJet works wonders."

Swiffer WetJet is the safe, easy way to clean your wood floors. Our wood solution reveals natural beauty without damage or dulling. The super-absorbent pad locks away 3× more dirt and solution than any other pad. And dosing control means no over-soaking. So cleaning with WetJet is faster, easier, simpler, drier and better. Which is so very Swiffer. www.wetjet.com

B

Simple as ABC

A. Squeeze the trigger
B. Release the cleaner, no need for buckets
C. Toss the pad, dirt and all

Sparkling clean floors, even wood floors, in half the time. Clorox™ Readymop™ all-in-one mopping system.

What could be simpler?

www.readymop.com

EXAMPLE 17

Size/color: Both ads were 1-page, 4-color ads.

Test magazines: Ad A—*People,* Spring

Ad B—*People,* Winter

Magazine type: *People* focuses on compelling personalities of our time, from the known to the unknown, the famous to the infamous, the ordinary to the extraordinary. Likewise the publication serves as a guide to important developments in the arts, sciences, politics, sports, television, motion pictures, books, and records, with the spotlight on people involved in those areas.

Assignment: Which ad performed better among women and why do you think so?

STUDENT ANALYSIS

NAME _____ CLASS _____ DATE _____

EXAMPLE 18

Courtesy of DHL.

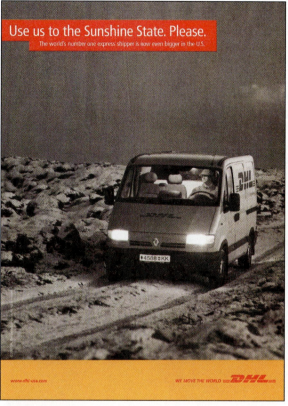

Courtesy of DHL.

A

Yellow.

It's the new brown.

Discover a new color with a new attitude that's going to change the way America ships. DHL is now bigger than ever, better than ever and hungry for your business. Call 1-800-CALL DHL to find out how yellow is going to give brown a run for its money.

www.dhl.com

We move the world DHL

B

Use us to the Sunshine State. Please. The world's number one express shipper is now even bigger in the U.S.

www.dhl-usa.com

We move the world DHL

EXAMPLE 18

Size/color:	Both ads were 1-page, 4-color ads.
Test magazines:	Ad A—*People,* Fall
	Ad B—*People,* Spring
Magazine type:	*People* focuses on compelling personalities of our time, from the known to the unknown, the famous to the infamous, the ordinary to the extraordinary. Likewise the publication serves as a guide to important developments in the arts, sciences, politics, sports, television, motion pictures, books, and records, with the spotlight on people involved in those areas.
Assignment:	Which ad performed better among women and why do you think so?

STUDENT ANALYSIS

NAME_____ CLASS_____ DATE_____

EXAMPLE 19

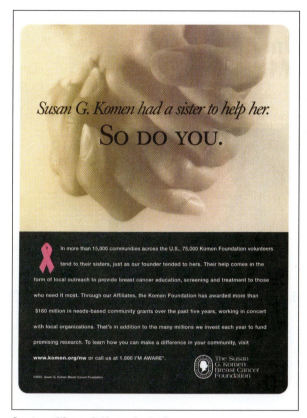

Courtesy of Susan G. Komen for the Cure.

Courtesy of Susan G. Komen for the Cure.

A

Susan G. Komen had a sister to help her.

So do you.

In more than 15,000 communities across the U.S., 75,000 Komen Foundation volunteers tend to their sisters, just as our founder tended to hers. Their help comes in the form of local outreach to provide breast cancer education, screening and treatment to those who need it most. Through our Affiliates, the Komen Foundation has awarded more than $160 million in needs-based community grants over the past 5 years, working in concert with local organizations. That's in addition to the many millions we invest each year to fund promising research. To learn how you can make a difference in your community, visit www.komen.org/nw or call us at 1.800 I'M AWARE.®

The Susan G. Komen Breast Cancer Foundation

B

We can live without our hair.

We can live without our breasts.

We cannot live without our hope for a cure.

Support our Race against breast cancer. For more information, visit komen.org/lhj2 or call 1.888.603.RACE.

The Susan G. Komen Breast Cancer Foundation Race for the cure

EXAMPLE 19

Size/color:	Both ads were 1-page, 4-color ads.
Test magazines:	Ad A—*Newsweek,* Winter
	Ad B—*Ladies' Home Journal,* Spring
Magazine type:	*Newsweek* is a major newsweekly magazine, second only to *Time* in circulation. With bureaus world-wide, it covers both national and international news over a wide range of topics: political, governments, cultural, and technological. It also provides regular commentary and opinions on the major concerns of the week. Its content appeals to both men and women, as it reviews the important happenings of the week that affect our lives.
	Ladies' Home Journal contains highly focused features and articles that reflect varied interests such as beauty and fashion, food and nutrition, health and medicine, home decorating and design, parenting, and self-help.
Assignment:	Which ad performed better among women and why do you think so?

STUDENT ANALYSIS

NAME_____ CLASS_____ DATE_____

EXAMPLE 20

Pepsi Cola Company.

A

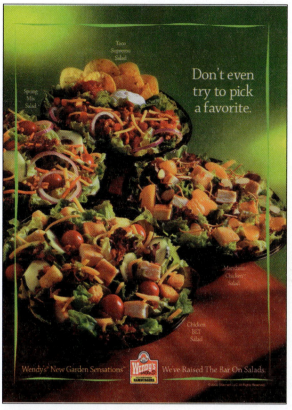

Courtesy of Wendy's International, Inc.

B

Experience the tropical lime storm.

New Mountain Dew Baja Blast, Only at Taco Bell.

www.DewBajaBlast.com

Think outside the bun

Taco Bell

Don't even try to pick a favorite.

Spring Mix Salad

Taco Supremo Salad

Mandarin Chicken™ Salad

Chicken BLT Salad

Wendy's® New Garden Sensations™

We've Raised The Bar On Salads.

EXAMPLE 20

Size/color: Both ads were 1-page, 4-color ads.

Test magazines: Both ads were tested in *People,* Summer

Magazine type: *People* focuses on compelling personalities of our time, from the known to the unknown, the famous to the infamous, the ordinary to the extraordinary. Likewise the publication serves as a guide to important developments in the arts, sciences, politics, sports, television, motion pictures, books, and records, with the spotlight on people involved in those areas.

Assignment: Which ad performed better among women and why do you think so?

STUDENT ANALYSIS

NAME_____ CLASS_____ DATE_____